MOROCCO
TRAVEL
GUIDE

Captivating Adventures through Whitewashed Beauty,

Local Culture, Moroccan Landmarks, Hidden Gems, and More

Welcome Aboard, Discover
Your Limited-Time Free Bonus!

Hello, traveler! Welcome to the Captivating Travels family, and thanks for grabbing a copy of this book! Since you've chosen to join us on this journey, we'd like to offer you something special.

Check out the link below for a FREE Ultimate Travel Checklist eBook & Printable PDF to make your travel planning stress-free and enjoyable.

But that's not all - you'll also gain access to our exclusive email list with even more free e-books and insider travel tips. Well, what are you waiting for? Click the link below to join and embark on your next adventure with ease.

Access your bonus here: https://livetolearn.lpages.co/checklist/
Or, Scan the QR code!

TABLE OF CONTENTS

Introduction   5

Chapter 1: Get to Know Morocco   11

Chapter 2: Arriving in Morocco   17

Chapter 3: Marrakech – The Red City   30

Chapter 4: Fes – The Cultural and Spiritual Heart   47

Chapter 5: The Sahara Desert – A Journey into the Dunes   58

Chapter 6: The Blue City of Chefchaouen   66

Chapter 7: Casablanca & Rabat – Modern Meets Tradition   77

Chapter 8: Essaouira – The Coastal Gem   88

Chapter 9: The High Atlas Mountains & Hidden Villages   97

Chapter 10: Moroccan Culture, Customs, and Etiquette   106

Chapter 11: Top 20 Must-See Locations in Morocco   113

Chapter 12: Best Places for Photography in Morocco   125

Bonus Chapter: Useful Moroccan Arabic (Darija)
                            Survival Phrases   133

Appendix: Quick Reference Guide to Key Locations   138

Here's another book by Captivating Travels
that you might like   142

Welcome Aboard, Discover Your Limited-Time
Free Bonus!   143

Image Sources   144

INTRODUCTION

Welcome to Morocco, a land of awe-inspiring landscapes, rich history, and vibrant culture. From the bustling souks of Marrakech to the endless golden dunes of the Sahara, Morocco offers an adventure unlike any other. Whether you're wandering through the blue-washed streets of Chefchaouen, tasting fragrant spices in Fes, or exploring the ancient kasbahs of the Atlas Mountains, this North African gem captivates every traveler.

The Saadian Pavilion at the Menara Gardens of Marrakech, Morocco

Map view of Morocco[1]

WHY VISIT MOROCCO?

Morocco is a country of **contrasts** — where modernity and tradition intertwine seamlessly. Here, you'll find ancient medinas alongside contemporary cafes, camel caravans crossing the desert, and luxury riads offering world-class hospitality.

Some highlights of Morocco include:

✦ **Diverse Landscapes** – From mountains to beaches to deserts, Morocco has it all.

✦ **Rich Culture & Traditions** – Experience the warmth of Moroccan hospitality, music, and festivals.

✦ **Incredible Architecture** – Discover intricate palaces, mosques, and kasbahs.

✦ **World-Famous Cuisine** – Taste dishes like tagine, couscous, and fresh mint tea.

✦ **Exciting Adventures** – Trek the Atlas Mountains, ride camels in the Sahara, or surf in Essaouira.

The old city of Essaouira in Morocco

Scan the QR code for an interactive map of Morocco.

HOW TO USE THIS GUIDE

Spices sold at a market in Morocco

This travel guide is designed to help you explore Morocco with ease. You'll find:

✦ **City and region highlights** – What to see, do, and eat in each destination.

✦ **Cultural insights** – Learn about customs, etiquette, and local traditions.

✦ **Practical tips** – Information on transportation, safety, and the best time to visit.

✦ **Detailed maps** – To help you navigate Morocco's streets and landscapes.

✦ **QR codes for navigation** – Scan and get instant access to locations, travel routes, and recommendations.

✦ **Colorful images** – Stunning photos that bring Morocco's beauty to life.

The blue city of Chefchaouen

Tourists standing at the peak of Mount Toubkal, Morocco

Morocco is **a year-round destination**. Here's what you can look forward to in every season:

✦ **Spring (March-May):** Pleasant weather, lush landscapes, and fewer crowds.

✦ **Fall (September-November):** Ideal for desert excursions and city explorations.

✦ **Summer (June-August):** Coastal cities are great, but the inland can be very hot.

✦ **Winter (December-February):** Snow in the mountains, while the desert remains cool and magical.

READY TO EXPLORE?

Make the most of your visit to Morocco

Morocco is waiting for you! Whether you're seeking adventure, relaxation, or cultural immersion, this guide — filled with **detailed maps, QR codes for easy navigation, and vibrant color photos**—will help you plan the perfect trip. **Let's begin your journey through Morocco!**

Scan the QR Code for more information about Morocco tourism centres.

1

GET TO KNOW MOROCCO

A LAND OF DIVERSITY AND RICH HISTORY

> Morocco is a country of vivid contrasts—where ancient traditions meet modern influences, and natural landscapes range from sweeping deserts to lush valleys. Nestled in North Africa, Morocco shares borders with Algeria, the Atlantic Ocean, and the Mediterranean Sea, offering travelers an array of stunning backdrops.

With a history shaped by Berber, Arab, and European influences, Morocco's heritage is as **diverse as its landscapes**. From the grandeur of imperial cities like Marrakech and Fes to the remote beauty of the Sahara, every corner of Morocco has a story to tell.

The Complex of Hasan II mosque in Casablanca

GEOGRAPHY: FROM MOUNTAINS TO DESERTS

The Atlas Mountains of Morocco

Morocco's landscapes are as **varied as its culture**, making it a dream destination for all types of travelers.

✦ **The Atlas Mountains** – Stretching across the country, these mountains are home to Berber villages, deep valleys, and even **snow-capped peaks** in winter. Mount Toubkal, North Africa's highest peak, is a must for hikers.

✦ **The Sahara Desert** – The golden dunes of **Erg Chebbi and Erg Chigaga** offer unforgettable experiences, from camel treks to nights under a starry sky.

✦ **The Mediterranean & Atlantic Coasts** – Cities like Tangier, Essaouira, and Agadir boast beautiful beaches, fresh seafood, and a laid-back coastal vibe.

✦ **The Imperial Cities** – **Marrakech, Fes, Meknes, and Rabat** showcase Morocco's rich history through palaces, mosques, and vibrant markets.

✦ **The Hidden Valleys and Oases** – The Dades and Todra Gorges, along with lush palm-filled valleys like the **Ziz Valley**, offer breathtaking scenery and a glimpse of traditional Berber life.

Traditional kasbah houses seen in Ziz Valley

A BRIEF HISTORY OF MOROCCO

Volubilis, a UNESCO World Heritage Site

Morocco's past is a blend of **Berber, Arab, and European** influences, shaped by centuries of trade, conquest, and culture.

✦ **Ancient Berber Roots (Pre-7th Century):** The indigenous Berbers, also known as Amazigh, have lived in Morocco for thousands of years, leaving behind fascinating traditions and architectural wonders.

- ✦ **The Arrival of Islam (7th Century):** Arab influence introduced Islam, shaping Morocco's culture, architecture, and way of life.

- ✦ **The Great Dynasties (11th-17th Century):** Powerful rulers, including the Almoravids and the Saadians, built iconic cities, mosques, and kasbahs.

- ✦ **European Influence & Independence (19th-20th Century):** After a period of French and Spanish colonization, Morocco gained independence in 1956 and has since thrived as a unique blend of old and new.

MOROCCAN CULTURE AND DAILY LIFE

A woman serves tea with the Moroccan landscape in the background

Moroccan culture is **deeply rooted in tradition**, with influences from **Islam, Berber heritage, and centuries of global connections**. Here's what makes it special:

1. LANGUAGE & COMMUNICATION

- ✦ The official languages are **Arabic and Berber (Amazigh)**, but **French is widely spoken** in business and tourism.

- ✦ **Moroccan Arabic (Darija)** is different from standard Arabic, with a mix of Berber, French, and Spanish influences.

- ✦ In cities, many people speak **English**, especially in tourist areas.

2. HOSPITALITY & SOCIAL NORMS

✦ **Tea is a symbol of hospitality.** If invited for tea, accept it — it's a sign of friendship!

✦ **Greetings are warm and personal.** A handshake and a smile go a long way, and friends may kiss on both cheeks.

✦ **Respect for elders is important.** It's customary to greet older people first in a group setting.

3. RELIGION & TRADITIONS

✦ Morocco is **a Muslim-majority country**, and Islamic traditions shape daily life.

✦ **The call to prayer (adhan)** is heard five times a day from mosques.

✦ **During Ramadan,** many restaurants close during the day, and fasting is widely observed.

MUST-TRY MOROCCAN EXPERIENCES

A traditional souk filled with treasures to shop during your visit to Morocco[2]

To truly understand Morocco, you have to **experience its traditions, flavors, and natural wonders**. Here are some must-try activities:

- ✦ **Explore the souks and markets** – Get lost in the lively markets of Fes, Marrakech, and Chefchaouen.

- ✦ **Ride a camel in the Sahara** – Experience the magic of the desert on a traditional camel trek.

- ✦ **Visit a traditional hammam** – A Moroccan bathhouse offers a relaxing and cultural spa experience.

- ✦ **Taste Moroccan cuisine** – Try dishes like tagine, pastilla, harira soup, and fresh mint tea.

- ✦ **Stay in a riad** – These beautiful courtyard homes turned guesthouses offer an authentic Moroccan stay.

YOUR MOROCCAN JOURNEY BEGINS

Now that you have a glimpse of Morocco's landscapes, history, and culture, it's time to **dive into the details**. In the next chapters, we'll explore Morocco's top destinations, how to navigate the country, and hidden gems you won't want to miss. **Your adventure starts now!**

2

ARRIVING IN MOROCCO

ENTRY REQUIREMENTS AND VISAS

> Morocco is a welcoming destination, but travelers should be aware of entry requirements before their trip.

✦ **Visa-Free Entry:** Citizens from the **United States, Canada, the United Kingdom, the European Union, Australia, and several other countries** can enter Morocco without a visa for up to **90 days**.

The exterior of Marrakesh Airport

- ✦ **Visa Required:** Travelers from some countries must apply for a visa in advance through a Moroccan consulate or embassy.

- ✦ **Passport Requirements:** Your passport must be valid for at least **six months beyond your date of entry**. Ensure you have at least **one blank page** for entry and exit stamps.

- ✦ **Customs Regulations:** Travelers can bring **reasonable amounts of personal items, electronics, and currency**, but large sums of cash over **100,000 Moroccan dirhams (MAD)** must be declared.

Check with the Moroccan consulate in your country
before traveling, as entry rules may change.
Scan the QR Code for more information.

MAIN INTERNATIONAL AIRPORTS

Morocco has several international airports, each serving different regions and types of travelers. Most international flights arrive from **Europe, the Middle East, Africa, and North America**.

1. MOHAMMED V INTERNATIONAL AIRPORT (CMN) – CASABLANCA

Mohammed V International Airport[3]

✦ The **largest and busiest** airport in Morocco, handling most long-haul flights.

✦ Ideal for travelers flying from **North America, the Middle East, and sub-Saharan Africa**.

✦ The airport has **modern facilities**, duty-free shops, lounges, and currency exchange services.

✦ Transportation:

○ **Train:** A railway station inside the airport connects to Casablanca's city center and other major cities.

○ **Taxis:** A taxi to downtown Casablanca costs **250-350 MAD**.

○ **Car rentals:** Available from international and local companies.

2. MARRAKECH MENARA AIRPORT (RAK) – MARRAKECH

Menara Airport in Marrakech

✦ One of Morocco's busiest airports, popular with tourists visiting **Marrakech, the Atlas Mountains, and the desert**.

✦ Many flights arrive from **Europe**, with several low-cost airlines operating routes to Marrakech.

✦ Facilities include **cafés, duty-free shops, and lounges**.

✦ Transportation:

○ **Taxis:** The main way to reach the city, costing **100-150 MAD**.

○ **Bus:** Bus 19 connects the airport to the medina and central areas.

○ **Car rentals:** Good for those planning to drive to the surrounding areas.

3. FÈS–SAÏSS AIRPORT (FEZ)

FEZ Airport[4]

+ Best for travelers exploring **Fes, Meknes, and northern Morocco**.

+ Flights mostly arrive from **Europe and the Middle East**, with some seasonal routes.

+ A smaller airport but offers essential services like **currency exchange and car rentals**.

+ Transportation:

  ○ **Taxis:** The most convenient option, with fares around **120-180 MAD**.

  ○ **Shuttle bus:** A budget-friendly option costing **20-50 MAD**.

4. TANGIER-IBN BATTOUTA INTL. AIRPORT (TNG) – TANGIER

Map view of Tangier Ibn Battouta Airport[5]

✦ Serves travelers heading to **northern Morocco, including Tangier, Chefchaouen, and Tetouan**.

✦ Convenient for those arriving from **Spain and Portugal**, with short flights from Madrid, Barcelona, and Lisbon.

✦ Small but efficient, with basic facilities and a few shops and restaurants.

✦ Transportation:

    ○ **Taxis:** A ride to Tangier city center costs around **100-150 MAD**.

    ○ **Rental cars:** A great option for exploring the northern region.

5. RABAT-SALÉ AIRPORT (RBA) – RABAT

Rabat-Salé Airport[6]

✦ The **smallest** of Morocco's major international airports, serving the capital city.

✦ Mostly used for flights within **Europe and North Africa**.

✦ Limited but functional services, including car rentals and currency exchange.

✦ Transportation:

  ○ **Taxis:** A trip to Rabat costs **150-200 MAD**.

  ○ **Shuttle bus:** Runs to the city at a lower cost.

6. AGADIR AL-MASSIRA INTERNATIONAL AIRPORT (AGA) – AGADIR

Map view of Agadir Al-Massira International Airport[7]

✦ Best for travelers heading to **Agadir, Taghazout, and the southern Atlantic coast**.

✦ Popular for **beach vacations and surfing trips**.

✦ Mainly serves flights from **Europe and domestic routes from Casablanca**.

✦ Transportation:

    ○ **Taxis:** The fastest way to reach Agadir, with fares around **200-300 MAD**.

    ○ **Car rentals:** Useful for travelers exploring the coastal region.

7. OUARZAZATE AIRPORT (OZZ) – OUARZAZATE

Ouarzazate International Airport

✦ A small airport serving the **gateway to the Sahara Desert and the Atlas Mountains**.

✦ Primarily handles **domestic flights and seasonal European routes**.

✦ Transportation:

○ **Taxis:** Available to take travelers to the city center and surrounding kasbahs.

○ **Car rentals:** Recommended for those venturing into the desert.

GETTING FROM THE AIRPORT TO THE CITY

Once you land, there are several ways to get from the airport to your destination.

1. TAXIS

Taxis are available at all major airports, but they do not always use meters. It's best to **agree on a price before getting in**. Here are estimated fares:

- **Casablanca Airport to city center:** 250-350 MAD
- **Marrakech Airport to medina:** 100-150 MAD
- **Fes Airport to city center:** 120-180 MAD
- **Tangier Airport to city center:** 100-150 MAD

2. AIRPORT SHUTTLES AND BUSES

Many airports offer bus services to the city center at a lower cost.

- **Casablanca:** Train service from the airport to the city center runs every hour.
- **Marrakech:** Bus 19 connects the airport to the medina.
- **Fes and Tangier:** Shuttle buses run to the city for around **20-50 MAD**.

3. CAR RENTALS

For travelers planning to drive, rental cars are available at all major airports. Roads in Morocco are well-maintained, but traffic in big cities can be **chaotic**. Renting a car is best for trips to remote areas like the **Atlas Mountains and the Sahara Desert**.

ARRIVING BY FERRY

A view from a ferry in Tangier

For travelers coming from **Spain**, ferries provide a convenient way to enter Morocco.

✦ **Most ferries depart from Algeciras or Tarifa (Spain) and arrive at the Port of Tanger or in Tangier Ville.**

✦ The trip takes **1-2 hours**, with multiple departures daily.

✦ Passports are stamped **onboard the ferry**, so make sure to arrive early to complete immigration procedures.

MONEY AND CURRENCY EXCHANGE

The official currency of Morocco is the **Moroccan dirham (MAD)**.

+ **Exchange Rates:** 1 USD ≈ 10 MAD (rates may vary*).
+ **ATMs:** Widely available in cities and towns. They accept **Visa, Mastercard, and other major cards**.
+ **Currency Exchange:** Available at airports, banks, and exchange offices. Airports usually have **higher fees** than city exchange offices.
+ **Credit Cards:** Accepted in hotels, restaurants, and larger stores but **cash is preferred in markets and small shops**.

LOCAL SIM CARDS AND INTERNET ACCESS

Staying connected in Morocco is easy, with **affordable mobile data and Wi-Fi in most hotels and cafes**.

+ **Best SIM Card Providers:** Maroc Telecom, Orange, Inwi.
+ **Cost:** A prepaid SIM with **5GB of data costs around 50-100 MAD**.
+ **Where to Buy:** Available at the airport, mobile stores, and kiosks in major cities.

SAFETY AND TRAVEL TIPS

+ **Scams and Overcharging:** Be cautious in tourist areas where some vendors and taxi drivers may overcharge. Always **negotiate prices in markets and confirm taxi fares in advance**.
+ **Pickpocketing:** Like any tourist destination, pickpocketing can occur in crowded areas. Keep your valuables secure.
+ **Local Laws:** Morocco is a Muslim country, and certain behaviors—such as public intoxication and drug use—are illegal. Dress modestly in rural areas and religious sites.

NEXT STEPS IN YOUR JOURNEY

A group of friends enjoying their visit to Morocco[8]

Now that you have arrived in Morocco, it's time to explore its most fascinating destinations. In the next chapters, we'll take you through the streets of Marrakech, the historical wonders of Fes, and the golden sands of the Sahara.

3

MARRAKECH – THE RED CITY

Marrakech is one of Morocco's most vibrant and historic cities. Known as the Red City because of its terracotta-colored buildings, it is a place where ancient traditions, bustling markets, and modern luxury blend seamlessly. From the maze-like medina to the stunning palaces and gardens, Marrakech offers an unforgettable experience for every traveler.

Jemaa el-Fnaa in Marrakech

Map view of Marrakech[9]

A BRIEF HISTORY OF MARRAKECH

El Badi Palace

Founded in **1062** by the Almoravid dynasty, Marrakech quickly became a powerful imperial city. It was a key center for **trade, culture, and Islamic scholarship**, attracting merchants and scholars from across Africa, the Middle East, and Europe. Over the centuries, Marrakech has been shaped by different rulers, leaving behind **stunning palaces, mosques, and gardens** that still define the city today.

1. JEMAA EL-FNAA: THE HEART OF MARRAKECH

A horse-drawn carriage seen at Jemaa el-Fnaa

At the center of Marrakech's medina is **Jemaa el-Fnaa**, a **UNESCO World Heritage Site** and one of the most famous squares in the world. During the day, it is filled with **fresh juice vendors, henna artists, snake charmers, and horse-drawn carriages** offering rides through the old city. In the evening, the square transforms into a lively **food market with traditional Moroccan dishes, street performers, and live music**.

✦ **Must-Do:** Try fresh orange juice, watch a traditional storyteller, take a **calèche (horse-drawn carriage) ride** around the medina, and enjoy a bowl of harira soup from a local stall.

✦ **Best View:** Head to a rooftop café for a panoramic view of the square, especially at sunset.

Be sure to try a glass of refreshing orange juice at the square

2. THE SOUKS: A SHOPPER'S PARADISE

Shoes for sale at a souk

Marrakech's **souks (markets)** are among the most famous in Morocco. Located north of Jemaa el-Fnaa, they are a labyrinth of narrow alleyways filled with **handmade crafts, carpets, leather goods, spices, and jewelry**.

Must-Do:

✦   Visit the **Souk Semmarine** for colorful textiles and ceramics.

✦   Explore the **Souk el Attarine** for perfumes and spices.

✦   Watch artisans making **leather goods in Souk Cherratine**.

Bargaining Tip: Haggling is expected in the souks. Start by offering **half the initial price** and negotiate with a smile.

Scan the QR Code for an interactive map of souk markets.

HISTORIC PALACES AND ARCHITECTURAL WONDERS

3. BAHIA PALACE

Bahia Palace gardens

A **19th-century masterpiece**, the Bahia Palace was built for the grand vizier of Marrakech. It features **stunning courtyards, intricate tilework, and beautiful gardens**, offering a glimpse into the opulent lifestyle of Moroccan royalty.

✦   **Best Time to Visit:** Early morning to avoid crowds.

✦   **Entrance Fee:** Around **70 MAD**.

4. EL BADI PALACE

El Badi Palace

Once a **lavish palace**, El Badi now stands as an impressive ruin. Built in the **16th century by Sultan Ahmad al-Mansur**, it was once decorated with gold, marble, and onyx. Today, visitors can explore its **vast courtyards and underground passageways**.

✦ **Must-Do:** Climb to the **rooftop terrace** for views of the city.

✦ **Entrance Fee:** Around **70 MAD**.

5. KOUTOUBIA MOSQUE

Koutoubia Mosque

Marrakech's largest mosque, the **Koutoubia,** is a striking landmark with a towering **77-meter minaret**. Built in the **12th century**, it inspired the design of the Hassan Tower in Rabat and La Giralda in Seville.

✦ **Non-Muslims cannot enter**, but the mosque can be admired from the outside.

✦ **Best Photo Spot:** Visit at sunset when the mosque glows against the sky.

6. MAJORELLE GARDEN & YVES SAINT LAURENT MUSEUM

The Majorelle Garden

Originally designed by **French artist Jacques Majorelle** and later restored by fashion icon **Yves Saint Laurent**, this garden is an oasis in the city. It features exotic plants, fountains, and the famous **blue-painted villa**.

Entrance Fee:

✦ **Majorelle Garden:** Around **150 MAD**

✦ **YSL Museum:** Around **100 MAD**

TIP:

Tickets sell out quickly—buy them online in advance.

You can visit the Yves Saint Laurent Museum at the Majorelle Garden[10]

Scan the QR Code for more details about this setting.

7. THE SECRET GARDEN

The Secret Garden

Located in the medina, the Secret Garden is a beautifully restored **Islamic garden** hidden behind high walls. It offers a peaceful retreat from the city's busy streets.

Must-Do: Climb the tower for **aerial views of the medina**.

Entrance Fee: Around **80 MAD**.

8. THE ATLAS MOUNTAINS & IMLIL VILLAGE

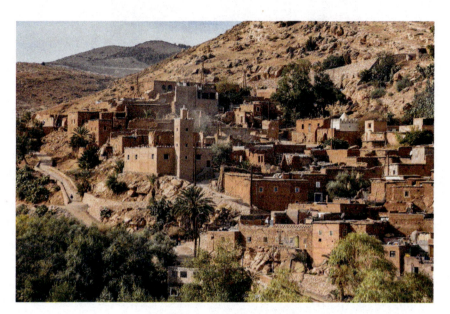

Imlil Village in the Atlas Mountains

Just a **1.5-hour drive** from Marrakech, the Atlas Mountains offer beautiful landscapes and Berber villages. Imlil is a popular starting point for **hiking Mount Toubkal**, the highest peak in North Africa.

✦ **Must-Do:** Have traditional **mint tea with a local Berber family**.

✦ **Best Time to Visit:** Spring and autumn for mild weather.

9. AIT BEN HADDOU: THE FAMOUS KASBAH

Ait Ben Haddou

Ait Ben Haddou is a **UNESCO-listed fortified village** made of red clay. It has been used as a filming location for movies like **Gladiator and Game of Thrones**. Located **three hours from Marrakech**, it makes for an exciting day trip.

✦ **Tip:** Go early to avoid tour groups.

✦ **Entrance Fee:** Ait Ben Haddou is technically free to visit, but residents may ask for a small payment (10 MAD) to help with preserving the structures.

10. OUZOUD WATERFALLS

Tourists enjoy the view at the Ouzoud Waterfalls

The **Ouzoud Waterfalls**, located **2.5 hours from Marrakech**, are the highest waterfalls in Morocco. Visitors can take a **boat ride**, swim in the pools, and spot wild monkeys.

Best Time to Visit: Spring and early summer when the water flow is strongest.

FOOD AND CULINARY EXPERIENCES IN MARRAKECH

11. MUST-TRY DISHES

A hearty Moroccan breakfast served on a rooftop terrace in the High Atlas Mountains

Marrakech is famous for its rich and flavorful cuisine. Some must-try dishes include:

✦ **Tagine:** Slow-cooked stew with lamb, chicken, or vegetables.

✦ **Couscous:** A traditional dish served with meat and vegetables.

✦ **Tanjia:** A Marrakech specialty, cooked in clay pots for hours.

✦ **Pastilla:** A flaky pastry filled with spiced chicken or pigeon and dusted with cinnamon and sugar.

✦ **Fresh Mint Tea:** A symbol of Moroccan hospitality.

12. BEST PLACES TO EAT

✦ **Café des Épices:** A rooftop café with views of the souks.

✦ **Nomad:** A modern restaurant serving Moroccan dishes with a twist.

✦ **La Maison Arabe:** Known for its high-end Moroccan cuisine and cooking classes.

TIP:

Street food in Jemaa el-Fnaa is safe to eat but choose stalls with high customer turnover.

A traditional riad interior with swimming pool

13. BEST RIADS AND HOTELS

Staying in a **riad** (a traditional Moroccan guesthouse) is part of the Marrakech experience.

+ **Luxury:** Royal Mansour, La Mamounia

+ **Budget:** Riad Les Jardins Mandaline, Equity Point Hostel

+ **Mid-Range:** Riad Yasmine, Riad BE

TIP:

Riads in the medina offer an authentic experience, while hotels in **Gueliz (the modern city)** provide more Western comforts.

FINAL THOUGHTS ON MARRAKECH

La Mamounia

Marrakech is a city that awakens the senses. Whether you are **wandering through the souks, exploring historic palaces, or enjoying a rooftop sunset over Jemaa el-Fnaa**, there is always something new to discover. In the next chapter, we'll take you to **Fes, Morocco's cultural and spiritual heart**, where history and tradition are beautifully preserved.

4 FES – THE CULTURAL AND SPIRITUAL HEART

Fes is Morocco's oldest imperial city and a center of culture, history, and traditional craftsmanship. Known as the spiritual heart of Morocco, Fes is home to the world's oldest university, an enormous medieval medina, and some of the most beautiful Islamic architecture in North Africa. Walking through its narrow, winding streets feels like stepping back in time, where artisans still practice ancient crafts and donkeys replace cars in the traffic of daily life.

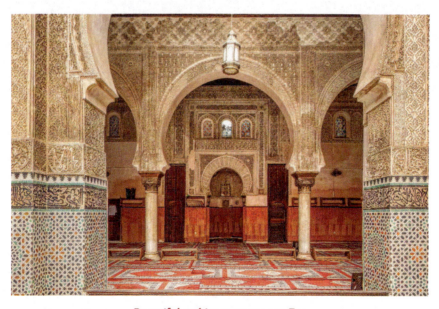

Beautiful architecture seen at Fes

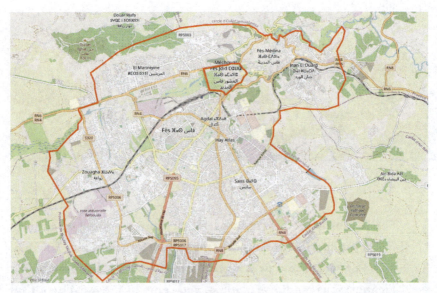

Map view of Fes[11]

A BRIEF HISTORY OF FES

Founded in **789 AD** by Idris I, the city of Fes quickly **a major center of learning and trade**. Over the centuries, it attracted scholars, artisans, and merchants from across the Islamic world.

During the **13th and 14th centuries**, under the rule of the **Marinid dynasty**, Fes reached its golden age and became the country's capital. Many of the city's stunning **madrasas (Islamic schools), mosques, and palaces** were built during this period, shaping the city's unique character.

Today, Fes remains one of the best-preserved medieval cities in the world, with a **UNESCO-listed medina** that has changed little over the centuries.

The Bab Bou Jeloud gate at Fes el Bali, A UNESCO World Heritage Site[12]

Scan the QR code for more information.

EXPLORING THE MEDINA: FES EL-BALI

The **medina of Fes el-Bali** is a labyrinth of over **9,000 alleyways**, making it one of the most **complex and authentic old cities** in the world. It is completely car-free, so the only way to explore is **on foot or by donkey**.

TIP:

The medina can be overwhelming for first-time visitors. Hiring a **local guide** is highly recommended.

1. UNIVERSITY OF AL-QARAWIYYIN AND MOSQUE

The historic university and mosque

Founded in **859 AD**, **al-Qarawiyyin** is recognized by UNESCO as the **oldest continuously operating university in the world**. It was a major center of Islamic learning, attracting scholars from across North Africa and the Middle East.

Non-Muslims cannot enter the mosque, but visitors can admire its **stunning courtyard and intricate tilework** from the entrance.

Scan the QR code for more information.

2. BOU INANIA MADRASA

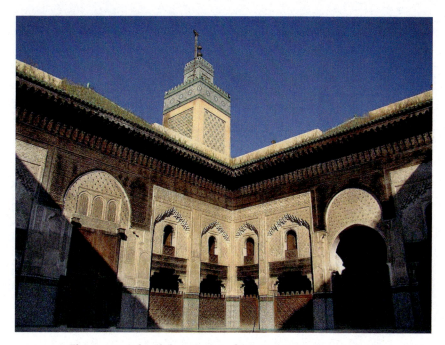

The courtyard and the minaret of Bou Inania Madrasa in Fes[13]

This **14th-century religious school** is one of the most beautifully decorated buildings in Fes. It features **intricate wood carvings, zellij tilework, and a large central courtyard**.

✦ **Visitors can enter for around 20 MAD** to explore the stunning architecture.

✦ **Best Time to Visit:** Morning or late afternoon for the best light and fewer crowds.

3. CHOUARA TANNERY

Chouara Tannery in Fes Morocco

One of the most famous sights in Fes, the **Chouara Tannery** has been producing **handmade leather** for centuries. Workers use traditional methods to dye and soften leather in large stone vats filled with natural ingredients like **pigeon droppings, saffron, and poppy flowers**.

✦ **Must-Do:** Visit a **leather shop terrace** for a **panoramic view** of the tannery.

TIP:

The smell can be strong—guides often provide **fresh mint leaves** to mask the scent.

4. NEJJARINE MUSEUM OF WOODEN ARTS & CRAFTS

The historic funduq where the Nejjarine Museum can be found

Housed in a beautifully restored **caravanserai (traders' inn)**, this museum showcases Morocco's **woodworking heritage**, including intricate **furniture, doors, and musical instruments**.

✦ **Great for history and architecture lovers.**

✦ **Entrance Fee:** Around **50 MAD**.

FES EL-JDID AND THE JEWISH QUARTER (MELLAH)

The main street of Fes el-Jdid[14]

Fes el-Jdid, or "New Fes," was built in the **13th century** as an extension of the old city. It is home to:

+ **The Royal Palace (Dar el-Makhzen):** Although not open to the public, its massive **bronze doors and intricate mosaics** make it one of the most photographed sites in Fes.

+ **The Jewish Quarter (Mellah):** Once home to Morocco's Jewish community, it features **distinctive balconies, synagogues, and a historic Jewish cemetery**.

Must-Visit: The **Ibn Danan Synagogue**, one of the oldest synagogues in North Africa.

DAY TRIPS FROM FES

5. MEKNES & VOLUBILIS

A perfect **day trip from Fes**, Meknes was once Morocco's capital and is known for its **grand gates, palaces, and imperial ruins**. Nearby, the **Roman ruins of Volubilis** offer a glimpse into Morocco's ancient past.

✦ **Travel Time: 1-hour drive** from Fes.

✦ **Must-See:** The well-preserved **mosaics and triumphal arch** at Volubilis.

6. SEFROU AND BHALIL

✦ **Sefrou:** A charming **Berber town with waterfalls and a laid-back atmosphere**.

✦ **Bhalil:** Known for its **cave houses**, where some locals still live in rock-carved homes.

Best for travelers looking for an authentic Moroccan village experience.

FOOD AND CULINARY EXPERIENCES IN FES

7. MUST-TRY DISHES

Bissara soup served with mint tea

Fes is known as the **gastronomic capital of Morocco**, famous for its **richly spiced and slow-cooked dishes**.

- ✦ **Bissara:** A thick **fava bean soup** served with olive oil and bread.
- ✦ **Pastilla:** A unique **sweet and savory pie** made with pigeon or chicken, almonds, and cinnamon.
- ✦ **Rfissa:** A comforting dish of **shredded msemen (Moroccan pancakes), lentils, and spiced chicken**.

8. BEST PLACES TO EAT

- ✦ **Dar Roumana:** Serves high-end Moroccan cuisine in a restored riad.

- ✦ **Cafe Clock:** A mix of Moroccan and international dishes, famous for its **camel burger**.

- ✦ **Riad Rcif:** Offers a luxurious **Fassi dining experience** with a multi-course meal.

TIP:
Many restaurants in the medina require reservations, especially for dinner.

WHERE TO STAY IN FES

9. BEST RIADS AND HOTELS

Staying in a **traditional riad** offers a more authentic experience than a hotel.

- ✦ **Luxury:** Riad Fes, Palais Amani

- ✦ **Mid-Range:** Dar Seffarine, Riad Laaroussa

✦ **Budget:** Dar Hafsa or Funky Fes Hostel

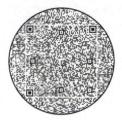 

TIP:

If staying inside the medina, ask your riad for **help with luggage**, as some areas are difficult to reach.

FINAL THOUGHTS ON FES

The famous Blue Gate

Fes is **Morocco's most historic city**, where ancient traditions remain alive in daily life. Whether you're wandering the medina, learning about the city's scholarly past, or enjoying its famous cuisine, Fes offers a **deep and immersive** cultural experience.

In the next chapter, we'll journey into the **Sahara Desert**, where rolling sand dunes, camel caravans, and starlit nights await.

5

THE SAHARA DESERT – A JOURNEY INTO THE DUNES

The Sahara Desert is one of Morocco's most awe-inspiring landscapes, offering an experience unlike any other. Stretching across North Africa, this vast expanse of golden dunes, rocky plateaus, and remote oases is a place of silence, beauty, and adventure. Whether you're riding a camel across the dunes, spending a night in a desert camp, or gazing at the Milky Way under a sky untouched by city lights, the Sahara is a journey every traveler to Morocco should take.

A caravan of camels seen in the Sahara desert

WHERE TO EXPERIENCE THE SAHARA IN MOROCCO

The **best places** to visit the Moroccan Sahara are **Erg Chebbi** and **Erg Chigaga**— two stunning dune regions offering different experiences.

Map view of the Sahara[15]

1. ERG CHEBBI – THE MOST ACCESSIBLE DUNES

A camp site in Erg Chebbi

Located near the town of **Merzouga**, **Erg Chebbi** features **towering sand dunes that reach up to 150 meters high**. It is the most famous and accessible part of the Moroccan Sahara, ideal for travelers with limited time.

✦ **Best For:** First-time desert visitors, those looking for luxury desert camps.

✦ **Getting There:** About **9 hours by car from Marrakech or 7 hours from Fes**.

✦ **Must-Do:** Ride a **camel at sunset**, sandboard down the dunes, and experience a **Berber music performance** by the campfire.

2. ERG CHIGAGA – THE WILD AND REMOTE SAHARA

Erg Chigaga

For a more **authentic, off-the-beaten-path** desert experience, head to **Erg Chigaga**, located near **M'Hamid**. These dunes are **more difficult to reach** but provide a true sense of desert isolation.

✦ **Best For:** Adventurers seeking a remote, untouched desert experience.

✦ **Getting There:** A **4x4 journey** from M'Hamid (about **10 hours from Marrakech**).

✦ **Must-Do:** Explore the desert on a **4x4 safari**, enjoy a traditional **nomadic tea ceremony**, and watch the **sunrise over the dunes**.

HOW TO GET TO THE SAHARA DESERT

Choose the transport option that works best for your budget

Reaching the Sahara requires **a long journey**, but the landscapes along the way make it an adventure in itself.

BY CAR (BEST FOR FLEXIBILITY)

Many travelers **rent a car or hire a driver** to explore at their own pace. The drive from Marrakech or Fes includes breathtaking stops such as:

✦ **Ait Ben Haddou (UNESCO Site):** An ancient kasbah featured in movies like *Gladiator* and *Game of Thrones*.

✦ **Dades and Todra Gorges:** Stunning rock formations perfect for hiking and photography.

✦ **Ziz Valley:** A lush oasis with thousands of date palm trees.

BY ORGANIZED TOUR (BEST FOR CONVENIENCE)

Several tour companies offer **3-day trips from Marrakech or Fes**, including transportation, accommodations, and activities. This is **a stress-free option** for those who don't want to drive.

TIP:

Choose a tour that includes **at least one night in the desert** to get the full experience.

BY BUS (BUDGET-FRIENDLY OPTION)

Overnight buses run from **Marrakech or Fes to Merzouga**, operated by **CTM and Supratours**. While this is the cheapest option, it's **less comfortable** than a private car or tour.

✦ **Travel Time: 10-12 hours**

✦ **Best For:** Solo travelers or those on a budget.

WHAT TO DO IN THE SAHARA DESERT

3. RIDE A CAMEL ACROSS THE DUNES

A camel ride in the Sahara is an unforgettable experience

Camel trekking is the most **iconic way to experience the desert**. The slow, swaying movement of the camel, the endless sand stretching in every direction, and the golden light of sunset create an unforgettable journey.

TIP:

Wear **long pants and a scarf** to protect yourself from the sun and sand.

4. SPEND A NIGHT IN A DESERT CAMP

A night in the desert is a must. Most camps offer:

✦ **Traditional Berber-style tents** made of wool and carpets.

✦ **Moroccan meals**, including tagine and fresh bread baked in the sand.

✦ **Live music and drumming** under the stars.

✦ **Luxury camps** with private bathrooms and comfortable beds for those seeking extra comfort.

✦ **Best Time to Visit:** Spring (March-May) and autumn (September-November) for cooler temperatures.

5. STARGAZING IN THE SAHARA

The Sahara is one of the **best places in the world for stargazing**, with no light pollution. On a clear night, you can see **thousands of stars, the Milky Way, and even shooting stars**.

TIP:

Bring a **tripod for night photography** if you want to capture the stars.

6. SANDBOARDING & 4X4 ADVENTURES

Conquer dunes of the Sahara with ease with the right transport

For thrill-seekers, many desert camps offer **sandboarding**, where you slide down dunes on a board. You can also take a **4x4 ride across the desert**, climbing dunes and exploring hidden oases.

Best Place: The **tall dunes of Erg Chebbi** are perfect for sandboarding.

7. MEET THE NOMADS OF THE SAHARA

The desert is home to **Amazigh (Berber) nomads**, who have lived here for centuries. Some tours offer **visits to nomadic families**, where you can learn about their **traditions, music, and way of life**.

Must-Try: Join a **traditional tea ceremony**, where mint tea is poured from high above the glass.

WHAT TO PACK FOR THE SAHARA

- **Loose, breathable clothing** to stay cool during the day.
- **A warm jacket** – Nights in the desert can be cold, especially in winter.
- **A scarf or turban** to protect against sand and sun.

- **Sunscreen, sunglasses, and lip balm** – The desert sun is strong.
- **Comfortable walking shoes** – Sandals are not ideal for hiking dunes.
- **A flashlight or headlamp** – Camps have limited electricity at night.

BEST TIME TO VISIT THE SAHARA

The desert has extreme temperatures, so choosing the right season is important.

BEST TIME:

- **Spring (March-May) and Autumn (September-November):** Warm days, cool nights, and clear skies.
- **Winter (December-February):** Cold nights, but pleasant daytime temperatures.

AVOID:

- **Summer (June-August):** Temperatures can exceed **45°C (113°F)**, making it too hot for most travelers.

FINAL THOUGHTS ON THE SAHARA DESERT

A camping site in the Sahara desert

A journey to the **Sahara Desert** is one of the most unforgettable experiences in Morocco. Whether you ride a camel across the dunes, enjoy the silence of the vast landscape, or gaze at the stars from your desert camp, this is a place that **stays with you long after you leave**.

In the next chapter, we'll travel to **Chefchaouen, the Blue City**, where winding streets, vibrant markets, and stunning mountain views await.

6

THE BLUE CITY OF CHEFCHAOUEN

Tucked away in the Rif Mountains, Chefchaouen is one of Morocco's most picturesque towns. Known as the Blue City, it is famous for its cobalt-colored streets, charming alleyways, and relaxed atmosphere. Unlike the bustling medinas of Marrakech and Fes, Chefchaouen offers a slower pace, making it an ideal stop for travelers looking to unwind and experience a different side of Morocco.

Chefchaouen

Map view of Chefchaouen[16]

WHY IS CHEFCHAOUEN BLUE?

The beautiful blue main square

One of the greatest mysteries of Chefchaouen is its **striking blue color**. While there are several theories, the most common explanations include:

✦ **Spiritual Significance:** Jewish refugees painted the town blue in the **15th century**, believing the color symbolized **heaven and spirituality**.

- ✦ **Mosquito Repellent:** Some locals say the blue paint helps keep **mosquitoes away**.
- ✦ **Tourism and Aesthetic Appeal:** In more recent years, the blue walls have become **an iconic attraction**, bringing travelers from around the world.

Whatever the reason, the **soothing shades of blue** make Chefchaouen one of Morocco's most **photogenic and peaceful** destinations.

EXPLORING CHEFCHAOUEN'S MEDINA

Chefchaouen's **medina (old town)** is **smaller and more relaxed** than those of Fes or Marrakech, making it easy to explore without feeling overwhelmed.

1. THE BLUE STREETS AND PHOTO SPOTS

An eye-catching blue door seen at Chefchaouen

Walking through Chefchaouen feels like stepping into a **dreamlike maze of blue alleyways, doorways, and staircases**. Some of the best **photo spots** include:

- **Place Outa el Hammam:** One of the **prettiest squares** with hanging flower pots and colorful rugs.

- **The Blue Staircase:** A famous **Instagram spot**, often decorated with plant pots and art.

- **Doors of Chefchaouen:** Many homes have **ornate blue doors** with beautiful patterns—perfect for photography.

TIP:

The **best time for photos** is early morning or late afternoon when the lighting is soft and the streets are quieter.

2. PLAZA UTA EL-HAMMAM

Plaza Uta el-Hammam pictured with the kasbah[17]

The **main square** of Chefchaouen, Plaza Uta el-Hammam, is the heart of the town. It is surrounded by **cafés, restaurants, and historical buildings**, making it the perfect place to relax and soak in the local atmosphere.

Must-Do: Enjoy a traditional **mint tea or fresh orange juice** at a café while people-watching.

3. THE KASBAH OF CHEFCHAOUEN

Located in the main square, the **Kasbah (fortress)** is a **15th-century** structure built by **Moulay Ali Ben Rachid**. It features **towers, Andalusian-style gardens, and a small museum** showcasing the history of Chefchaouen.

✦ **Best View:** Climb the **tower inside the kasbah** for a **panoramic view of the medina** and surrounding mountains.

✦ **Entrance Fee:** Around **60 MAD**, scan below QR Code for current pricing:

4. THE SPANISH MOSQUE

The Spanish Mosque

A short **hike uphill from the medina**, the **Spanish Mosque** offers **the best sunset view** in Chefchaouen. Built in the **1920s**, it was never actually used as a mosque, but today it serves as a **popular lookout point**.

✦ **Hike Duration:** About **30-40 minutes** from the medina.

✦ **Best Time to Go:** Late afternoon to catch the **sunset over the blue city**.

5. AKCHOUR WATERFALLS

Akchour Waterfalls

For nature lovers, a trip to **Akchour Waterfalls** is a **must-do**. Located **45 minutes from Chefchaouen**, these waterfalls offer **scenic hiking trails, natural pools, and lush greenery**.

✦ **Hike Duration: 2-3 hours round trip** (moderate difficulty).

✦ **Best Time to Visit:** Spring and autumn when the water flow is strong.

✦ **Must-Do:** Take a refreshing **swim in the natural pools**.

6. GOD'S BRIDGE

God's Bridge[18]

A **natural rock arch** formed over the Farda River, **God's Bridge** is another incredible hiking destination near Chefchaouen.

Hike Duration: 1.5-hour round trip (easy to moderate).

TIP:

Local guides are available for hire, but the trail is easy to follow on your own.

SHOPPING IN CHEFCHAOUEN

Colorful items for sale at Chefchaouen

Chefchaouen's markets are smaller and **less hectic** than those in Fes or Marrakech, making shopping **a more relaxed experience**.

Popular items to buy include:

+ **Wool blankets and rugs:** Handmade by local artisans in vibrant colors.

+ **Ceramics and pottery:** Blue-and-white designs inspired by the town's colors.

+ **Argan oil and rose products:** Natural beauty products sourced from Morocco.

+ **Leather goods:** The tanneries in Chefchaouen produce high-quality bags and shoes.

TIP:

Haggling is still part of the culture, but **prices are generally lower** than in bigger cities.

WHERE TO EAT IN CHEFCHAOUEN

While smaller than other Moroccan cities, Chefchaouen still offers some great **culinary experiences**.

7. MUST-TRY DISHES

A delicious Moroccan tagine

- ✦ **Bissara:** A **thick fava bean soup**, perfect for breakfast or a light meal.
- ✦ **Tagine Chefchaouen:** A local variation of **Moroccan tagine** made with regional spices.
- ✦ **Goat Cheese:** Chefchaouen is famous for its **locally produced goat cheese**, often served with olives and fresh bread.

8. BEST RESTAURANTS & CAFÉS

✦ **Casa Aladdin:** A rooftop restaurant with amazing **views of the medina**.

✦ **Bab Ssour:** Known for its **authentic Moroccan dishes** at reasonable prices.

✦ **Café Clock:** A great spot for travelers, offering **Moroccan food with a modern twist**.

TIP:

Many restaurants close **early**, so plan for an **early dinner**.

WHERE TO STAY IN CHEFCHAOUEN

Chefchaouen offers **a mix of riads, guesthouses, and budget-friendly hostels**.

✦ **Luxury:** Lina Ryad & Spa – Features a **hammam and panoramic views**.

✦ **Mid-Range:** Dar Echchaouen – A charming riad with a **pool and great location**.

✦ **Budget:** Riad Baraka – A cozy guesthouse perfect for **backpackers**.

TIP:

Staying **inside the medina** offers the most **authentic experience**, but hotels outside the medina **have better access to parking**.

BEST TIME TO VISIT CHEFCHAOUEN

+ **Spring (March-May) and Autumn (September-November):** The weather is **mild and perfect** for hiking.

+ **Winter (December-February):** Cooler, but the **blue tones of the city contrast beautifully with the misty mountains**.

AVOID: Summer (June-August): Hotter and **more crowded** with tourists.

FINAL THOUGHTS ON CHEFCHAOUEN

Clothing and ceramics on sale at Chefchaouen

Chefchaouen is a **peaceful and visually stunning** destination, offering a break from the fast-paced energy of Morocco's larger cities. Whether you are **wandering through the blue streets, hiking to waterfalls, or simply enjoying the relaxed atmosphere**, Chefchaouen is a place that **feels magical**.

In the next chapter, we'll explore **Casablanca and Rabat**, two cities where modernity and tradition come together.

CASABLANCA & RABAT – MODERN MEETS TRADITION

Casablanca and Rabat, Morocco's two largest coastal cities, offer a blend of modernity, history, and cultural richness. While Casablanca is the country's economic and business hub, Rabat serves as its political and administrative capital. Both cities showcase impressive architecture, coastal charm, and historical landmarks that make them worth exploring.

Map view of Casablanca[19]

Map view of Rabat[20]

CASABLANCA: MOROCCO'S COSMOPOLITAN CITY

Casablanca is Morocco's **largest city and financial center**, offering a glimpse into the country's **modern side**. While it may not have the medieval charm of Fes or Marrakech, it boasts **stunning colonial-era architecture, vibrant nightlife, and one of the most impressive mosques in the world**.

1. HASSAN II MOSQUE – A MODERN ARCHITECTURAL MARVEL

Hassan II Mosque

The **Hassan II Mosque** is **Casablanca's most famous landmark** and one of the largest mosques in the world. Completed in 1993, this stunning structure stands **partially over the Atlantic Ocean** and features **a towering minaret, intricate mosaics, and a retractable roof**.

Must-Do: Take a **guided tour** to explore the interior, as non-Muslims can only enter with a guide.

Entrance Fee: Around **130 MAD**.

Best Time to Visit: Early morning or late afternoon for the **best light and fewer crowds**.

2. THE CORNICHE – CASABLANCA'S SEASIDE PROMENADE

The Corniche waterfront

The **Corniche** is a long stretch of **beaches, cafés, and luxury hotels** along Casablanca's coastline. It's a great place for a **leisurely walk, sunset views, or enjoying fresh seafood** at one of the many restaurants.

✦ **Best Beaches:** Ain Diab and Lalla Meryem Beach.

✦ **Must-Do:** Enjoy a **coffee or meal** at a seaside café with **ocean views**.

3. THE ART DECO ARCHITECTURE OF CASABLANCA

Mohammed V Square[21]

Casablanca's **downtown area** is home to **beautiful Art Deco and colonial-era buildings**, a legacy of the city's French past. Key areas to explore include:

+ **Place Mohammed V:** The city's main square, surrounded by **stunning government buildings**.

+ **Boulevard Mohammed V:** A lively street lined with **historic theaters, hotels, and shops**.

4. THE OLD MEDINA – A GLIMPSE INTO THE PAST

While not as famous as Marrakech or Fes, Casablanca's **Old Medina** offers a look at the city's past. It's a **small but authentic** area filled with **local markets, traditional homes, and small cafés**.

Must-Do: Wander the narrow streets and visit **Rick's Café**, a restaurant inspired by the film *Casablanca*.

Rabat, located just **one hour north of Casablanca**, is Morocco's **capital and a UNESCO-listed city**. It is **cleaner, quieter, and more organized** than other major cities, offering a **mix of historic sites, modern boulevards, and coastal beauty**.

5. HASSAN TOWER & MAUSOLEUM OF MOHAMMED V

Hassan Tower

One of Rabat's most famous landmarks, **Hassan Tower** is an **unfinished minaret** from the 12th century. Nearby, the **Mausoleum of Mohammed V** houses the tombs of **King Mohammed V and his sons**, beautifully decorated with **white marble, zellij tilework, and golden ceilings**.

Entrance Fee: Free.

Best Time to Visit: Late afternoon for **soft lighting and fewer crowds**.

6. THE KASBAH OF THE UDAYAS

The Kasbah of the Udayas

Perched on a hill overlooking the Atlantic Ocean, the **Kasbah of the Udayas** is a **walled fortress** dating back to the 12th century. Inside, you'll find **narrow blue-and-white streets, stunning viewpoints, and peaceful gardens**.

+ **Must-Do:** Visit the **Andalusian Gardens** and enjoy a **traditional mint tea** at Café Maure.

+ **Best View:** From the kasbah's terrace, where you can see the **ocean and Rabat's coastline**.

7. RABAT'S MEDINA – A LOCAL SHOPPING EXPERIENCE

Rabat's **medina** is much **less chaotic** than those in Marrakech or Fes, making it **a pleasant place to shop for Moroccan crafts**. You'll find **handmade rugs, pottery, leather goods, and silver jewelry** at reasonable prices.

Best Shopping Streets: Rue des Consuls and Souk es Sebat.

TIP:

Prices are generally lower than in more tourist-heavy cities.

8. CHELLAH – THE ROMAN RUINS OF RABAT

Chellah

Chellah is a **fascinating archaeological site** that contains ruins from both the **Roman and Islamic periods**. Overgrown with plants and home to **storks nesting on ancient walls**, Chellah has a mystical, forgotten-city feel.

Must-Do: Walk through the ruins and explore the old **mosque, tombs, and Roman baths**.

Entrance Fee: Around **60 MAD**.

9. EL JADIDA – A PORTUGUESE COASTAL TOWN

El Jadida

About **1.5 hours south of Casablanca**, El Jadida is a **historic coastal town** known for its **Portuguese architecture, beaches, and relaxed atmosphere**.

Must-See: The **Portuguese Cistern**, a stunning underground water chamber with **arched ceilings and reflections of light**.

The Portuguese Cistern

10. SALE – THE TWIN CITY OF RABAT

The gallery around the courtyard of the Grand Mosque of Salé[22]

Located across the river from Rabat, **Salé** is often overlooked but offers an **authentic Moroccan experience**. It is known for its **historic medina, traditional mosques, and shipbuilding heritage**.

Must-Do: Visit the **Grand Mosque of Salé**, a historically significant Mosque originally constructed in 1028.

WHERE TO EAT IN CASABLANCA & RABAT

CASABLANCA

✦ **Rick's Café:** A replica of the café from *Casablanca*, serving Moroccan and international dishes.

✦ **La Sqala:** A beautiful garden restaurant offering **authentic Moroccan cuisine**.

- ✦ **Le Cabestan:** A high-end seafood restaurant with **ocean views**.

RABAT

- ✦ **Dar Rbatia:** A traditional Moroccan restaurant in a **beautiful riad setting**.

- ✦ **Le Dhow:** A unique dining experience on a **boat docked along the river**.

- ✦ **Al Marsa:** A stylish seafood restaurant at the **Rabat Marina**.

WHERE TO STAY IN CASABLANCA & RABAT

LUXURY:

- ✦ **Four Seasons Casablanca** – A **5-star hotel** with **oceanfront views**.

- ✦ **Sofitel Rabat Jardin des Roses** – A luxurious stay in **Rabat's embassy district**.

MID-RANGE:

- ✦ **Melliber Hotel Casablanca** – Great location near the **Hassan II Mosque**.

- **Riad Dar El Kebira (Rabat)** – A stunning riad with a **rooftop terrace**.

- **Riad Zyo (Rabat)** – A **modern yet traditional** riad with great service.

BUDGET:

- **Hotel Central (Casablanca)** – A charming **budget hotel** near the medina.

BEST TIME TO VISIT CASABLANCA & RABAT

- **Spring (March-May) and Fall (September-November):** The weather is **pleasant**, and the **coastal breeze keeps temperatures comfortable**.

- **Summer (June-August):** Warmer, but Casablanca and Rabat stay **cooler than inland cities**.

- **Winter (December-February):** Mild, with occasional rain.

FINAL THOUGHTS ON CASABLANCA & RABAT

While often overlooked in favor of Marrakech or Fes, Casablanca and Rabat offer a **unique mix of modern and historical experiences**. Whether you're admiring the grandeur of **Hassan II Mosque**, strolling through the **Kasbah of the Udayas**, or enjoying the coastal views, these cities provide **a different perspective on Morocco**.

In the next chapter, we'll explore **Essaouira – The Coastal Gem**, a laid-back beach town known for **windsurfing, seafood, and Portuguese forts**.

8

ESSAOUIRA - THE COASTAL GEM

Essaouira, a charming coastal town on Morocco's Atlantic coast, is known for its laid-back vibe, golden beaches, and rich history. With its whitewashed medina, vibrant blue fishing boats, and centuries-old ramparts, Essaouira is a refreshing contrast to Morocco's bustling inland cities. Once a major trading port, the town now attracts artists, musicians, and travelers looking to relax by the sea.

Unlike Marrakech or Fes, Essaouira offers **a slower pace of life**, making it a perfect destination to **unwind, explore, and enjoy fresh seafood**.

The fishing port of Essaouira

A BRIEF HISTORY OF ESSAOUIRA

The scenic Essaouira landscape[24]

Essaouira has long been a **strategic port** and trading center. The Phoenicians, Romans, and Portuguese all left their mark on the city before **Sultan Moham-med III** transformed it into a major **trade hub** in the 18th century. Known as **Mogador** until Morocco's independence, Essaouira became a meeting place for **merchants, musicians, and artisans from Africa, Europe, and the Middle East**.

Today, the Medina of Essaouira is a **UNESCO World Heritage Site**, preserving its mix of **Moroccan, European, and African influences**.

EXPLORING THE MEDINA

Essaouira's **medina** is much more **relaxed and easy to navigate** than those in Marrakech or Fes. It's filled with **craft shops, art galleries, and hidden cafés**, making it a wonderful place to **wander without stress**.

1. SKALA DE LA VILLE – THE OLD CITY WALLS

Skala de la Ville

Essaouira's **historic ramparts** were built in the **18th century** to protect the city from invaders. These thick stone walls, lined with **old bronze cannons**, offer **panoramic views of the Atlantic Ocean**.

✦ **Best Time to Visit:** Sunset, when the golden light makes for **stunning photographs**.

✦ **Must-Do:** Walk along the **ramparts**, featured in, among others, *Game of Thrones*.

2. MOULAY HASSAN SQUARE

Moulay Hassan Square

Essaouira's **main square** is a lively gathering spot surrounded by cafés, restaurants, and street performers. It's a great place to **relax with a coffee and watch daily life unfold**.

Must-Do: Visit in the evening when **local musicians** play live Gnawa music.

3. THE PORT AND BLUE FISHING BOATS

Essaouira's **working fishing port** is one of its most **iconic sights**. The docks are filled with **bright blue boats**, and fishermen sell their fresh catch directly from their stalls.

✦ **Must-Do:** Watch fishermen **repair their nets**, and try grilled seafood from one of the **portside stalls**.

✦ **Best Photo Spot:** The view of the **blue boats against the old city walls**.

4. ESSAOUIRA'S BEACHES & KITESURFING

Kitesurfing is a popular activity in the area

Essaouira's **long sandy beach** is perfect for **windsurfing, kitesurfing, and horseback riding**. The city's strong coastal winds make it **one of the best windsurfing spots in the world**.

Best Beaches:

✦ **Plage d'Essaouira:** The main beach, great for long walks and water sports.

✦ **Sidi Kaouki:** A more **secluded beach** popular with surfers.

Must-Do: Try **kitesurfing or windsurfing lessons**, available at several beach clubs.

5. A VISIT TO A WOMEN'S ARGAN OIL COOPERATIVE

Essaouira is famous for **argan oil**, a product unique to Morocco. Many local cooperatives, run by **Berber women**, offer **demonstrations on how argan oil is made**.

Must-Do: Visit a cooperative to see how **argan nuts are pressed into oil**, and buy **organic argan products** directly from the source.

6. HIKING IN THE THUYA FOREST

Just outside Essaouira, the **Thuya Forest** is home to unique Moroccan trees used for **woodworking and traditional crafts**. A short **hike or camel ride** through this peaceful forest is a great way to experience Morocco's natural beauty.

Must-Do: Visit a workshop where artisans craft **intricate wooden boxes and furniture**.

SHOPPING IN ESSAOUIRA

Woodwork items on sale at an Essaouira souk

Essaouira is known for its **art, music, and handicrafts**. Unlike in Marrakech, shopping here is **more relaxed**, with fairer prices and less haggling.

✦ **Woodwork & Thuya Crafts:** Hand-carved boxes, chessboards, and tables made from **Thuya wood**.

✦ **Argan Oil:** Essaouira is one of the best places to buy **pure, locally made argan oil**.

✦ **Silver Jewelry:** The city is known for its **handmade Berber and Tuareg jewelry. Traditional Textiles:** Wool rugs, scarves, and embroidered blankets are sold in the **medina's craft shops**.

TIP:

Visit the **Cooperative Artisanale des Marqueteurs** for quality, locally made crafts.

Delicious local seafood

Essaouira is famous for **seafood and Moroccan coastal cuisine**. Some must-try dishes include:

✦ **Grilled Sardines:** Freshly caught and served with lemon.

✦ **Seafood Tagine:** A flavorful mix of shrimp, calamari, and fish in Moroccan spices.

✦ **Couscous Bidaoui:** A variation of couscous made with lamb, beef, or vegetables.

BEST RESTAURANTS

✦ **Portside Seafood Stalls:** Choose fresh fish and have it grilled on the spot.

✦ **La Table by Madada:** A stylish restaurant known for its **seafood platters**.

✦ **Taros Café:** A rooftop restaurant with **ocean views and live music**.

TIP:

Essaouira has a strong **vegetarian-friendly food scene**, with plenty of **fresh salads, lentil dishes, and vegetarian tagines**.

WHERE TO STAY IN ESSAOUIRA

Essaouira offers a mix of **luxury hotels, charming riads, and budget-friendly guesthouses**.

✦ **Luxury:** Heure Bleue Palais – A stunning riad with a rooftop pool.

✦ **Mid-Range:** Riad Chbanate – A cozy, beautifully decorated riad in the medina.

✦ **Budget:** Riad Inna & Watersports Center – A budget-friendly stay near the beach.

TIP:

Stay **inside the medina** for an **authentic experience**, or **near the beach** if you plan to surf or kitesurf.

BEST TIME TO VISIT ESSAOUIRA

✦ **Spring (March-May) and Fall (September-November):** Warm temperatures and fewer tourists.

✦ **Summer (June-August):** The **windiest season**, perfect for **windsurfing and kitesurfing**.

✦ **Winter (December-February):** Cooler but still pleasant, with **fewer crowds**.

FINAL THOUGHTS ON ESSAOUIRA

A daytime scene in Essaouira

✦ Essaouira is a **perfect mix of history, nature, and relaxation**. Whether you're exploring the **blue fishing port, listening to Gnawa music in the medina, or riding a horse along the beach**, the city's **coastal charm is unforgettable**.

✦ In the next chapter, we'll head to **the High Atlas Mountains & Hidden Villages**, where adventure and traditional Berber culture await.

CHAPTER

9

THE HIGH ATLAS MOUNTAINS & HIDDEN VILLAGES

The High Atlas Mountains stretch across Morocco, offering some of the country's most dramatic landscapes, traditional Berber villages, and incredible outdoor adventures. This region is a paradise for hikers, nature lovers, and those seeking an authentic cultural experience. From snow-capped peaks to hidden valleys, the High Atlas is a world away from Morocco's bustling cities.

Whether you want to **trek to Mount Toubkal, explore remote Berber communities, or simply enjoy the fresh mountain air**, this chapter will guide you through the best experiences in the **High Atlas Mountains and its hidden villages**.

A group of people mountaintrekking in the High Atlas Mountains

EXPLORING THE HIGH ATLAS MOUNTAINS

The **High Atlas** is the tallest mountain range in North Africa, with peaks rising above **4,000 meters (13,000 feet)**. The region is home to **Berber (Amazigh) communities**, who have lived here for centuries, preserving their **language, traditions, and way of life.**

BEST TIME TO VISIT:

✦ **Spring (March-May):** Snow begins to melt, and the valleys turn lush and green.

✦ **Autumn (September-November):** Perfect weather for hiking and village exploration.

✦ **Winter (December-February):** Snowfall covers the peaks, and **Oukaïmeden becomes a skiing destination**.

1. IMLIL & MOUNT TOUBKAL – MOROCCO'S HIGHEST PEAK

Imlil Village

Imlil is a **small mountain village and the gateway to Mount Toubkal**, the highest peak in North Africa at **4,167 meters (13,671 feet)**. It's a popular base for trekkers and a great place to experience **Berber hospitality**.

TREKKING TO MOUNT TOUBKAL

The highest peak of Mount Toubkal

Trek Duration: 2 days (moderate to difficult level).

✦ **Starting Point:** Imlil (1,740 meters above sea level).

✦ **Overnight Stay:** Toubkal Refuge, a basic mountain hut near the summit.

✦ **Must-Do:** Watch the **sunrise from the summit**, with breath-taking views of the Atlas range.

TIP:

Even if you're not hiking to the summit, **shorter hikes around Imlil** offer spectacular scenery.

EXPERIENCING BERBER CULTURE IN IMLIL

✦ **Stay in a traditional guesthouse** and enjoy home-cooked tagine.

✦ **Visit a local Berber market**, where villagers trade fresh produce and handmade crafts.

✦ **Try Berber tea**, a strong mint tea served with mountain herbs.

2. AÏT BOUGUEMEZ – THE HAPPY VALLEY

Aït Bouguemez

Known as the **Happy Valley**, Aït Bouguemez is one of the most **beautiful and least-visited** regions in the High Atlas. It's a place of **terraced fields, quiet villages, and breathtaking mountain scenery**.

Must-Do:

✦ Visit **Sidi Moussa**, an ancient granary with **panoramic views** of the valley.

✦ Take a **guided village walk** to learn about **traditional farming and Berber customs**.

✦ Stay in a **family-run guesthouse** for a true cultural experience.

Best Time to Visit: Spring and autumn for mild temperatures and clear skies.

3. AÏT BEN HADDOU – MOROCCO'S MOST FAMOUS KASBAH

Aït Ben Haddou

Aït Ben Haddou is one of Morocco's most **iconic and best-preserved kasbahs (fortified villages)**. This **UNESCO World Heritage Site** has been featured in films and TV shows such as *Gladiator* and *Game of Thrones*.

Must-Do:

✦ Walk through the **ancient mud-brick houses** and climb to the **hilltop granary** for the best views.

✦ Explore the **small art galleries and craft shops** inside the kasbah.

✦ Visit in the **early morning or late afternoon** to avoid crowds.

How to Get There: A 3.5-hour drive from Marrakech, often combined with a visit to **Ouarzazate**.

4. THE TODRA AND DADES GORGES – DRAMATIC CANYONS

The Dades Gorge

These two spectacular gorges are **among the most stunning natural wonders in Morocco**, with **towering cliffs, lush palm groves, and winding roads**.

✦ **Todra Gorge:** A **narrow canyon with 300-meter-high cliffs**, perfect for **hiking and rock climbing**.

✦ **Dades Gorge:** Famous for its **curvy mountain road** and dramatic rock formations.

Must-Do:

✦ Hike through the **Todra Gorge** and stop at **local villages along the way**.

✦ Drive the **winding Dades road**, one of the most scenic routes in Morocco.

✦ Visit a **traditional Berber home** and learn about daily life in the mountains.

Best Time to Visit: Spring and autumn for cooler temperatures.

5. OUZOUD WATERFALLS – MOROCCO'S TALLEST WATERFALLS

Located about **2.5 hours from Marrakech**, the **Ouzoud Waterfalls** are the **tallest in Morocco**, cascading down **over 110 meters**.

Must-Do:

✦ Hike to the **base of the falls** and take a **boat ride under the waterfall**.

✦ Spot **Barbary macaques** (wild monkeys) in the surrounding olive trees.

✦ Enjoy a **traditional Berber meal** at one of the riverside cafés.

Best Time to Visit: Spring and early summer, when the water flow is strongest.

6. OUKAÏMEDEN – SKI RESORT

Consider skiing at Oukaïmeden during your visit

Yes, you can ski in Morocco! Oukaï-meden is the country's **highest ski resort**, located **75 km from Marrakech** at an altitude of **2,600 meters**.

✦ **Best Time for Skiing:** December to February.

✦ **Must-Do:** Take a **ski lesson from local Berber instructors** and enjoy the **panoramic mountain views**.

TIP:

Ski equipment is available for rent, but it's **best to bring your own** if you want higher-quality gear.

WHERE TO STAY IN THE HIGH ATLAS

✦ **Luxury:** Kasbah Tamadot – A stunning retreat owned by Richard Branson, offering **luxury with mountain views**.

✦ **Mid-Range:** Douar Samra – A **cozy eco-lodge** in Imlil with traditional architecture.

✦ **Budget:** Gîte Tizi Mizik – A friendly **Berber guesthouse** perfect for hikers.

TIP:

Staying in **a family-run guesthouse** gives you a more **authentic cultural experience**, with home-cooked meals and Berber hospitality.

WHAT TO PACK FOR THE HIGH ATLAS

✦ **Comfortable hiking shoes** – Essential for exploring the rugged terrain.

✦ **Layers of clothing** – Mountain weather can change quickly.

✦ **A scarf or hat** – For sun protection during hikes.

✦ **A flashlight or headlamp** – Villages have limited street lighting at night.

✦ **Cash** – ATMs are rare in remote areas, so bring enough money for your stay.

FINAL THOUGHTS ON THE HIGH ATLAS MOUNTAINS

The **High Atlas Mountains** are a world apart from Morocco's busy cities, offering a chance to **experience nature, history, and traditional Berber culture**. Whether you're **hiking to remote villages, exploring ancient kasbahs, or admiring dramatic landscapes**, the High Atlas is a destination that **feels untouched by time**.

In the next chapter, we'll uncover **Moroccan culture, customs, and etiquette**, helping you navigate social norms and traditions during your travels.

CHAPTER

10 MOROCCAN CULTURE, CUSTOMS, AND ETIQUETTE

Morocco's culture is a blend of Arab, Berber, African, and European influences, shaped over centuries of trade, conquest, and tradition. Understanding Moroccan customs, social norms, and etiquette will help you connect with locals, show respect, and make your travels more enjoyable. This chapter will guide you through greetings, dress codes, dining etiquette, and key cultural traditions.

An elderly Berber man seen on the terrace of his home

1. GREETINGS AND SOCIAL NORMS

Moroccans are known for their **warm hospitality and strong sense of community**. Greetings are important, and interactions often start with a series of **questions about family, health, and well-being** before getting to the main topic.

HOW TO GREET PEOPLE IN MOROCCO

✦ **Men greeting men:** A handshake, sometimes followed by a light touch on the heart. Close friends may **kiss on both cheeks**.

✦ **Women greeting women:** A **kiss on both cheeks** (starting with the right) or a handshake.

✦ **Men and women:** A handshake **only if the woman initiates it**. Some women prefer a simple **nod and verbal greeting**.

COMMON ARABIC GREETINGS:

✦ **Salam alaikum** – "Peace be upon you" (Common greeting)

✦ **Wa alaikum salam** – "And peace be upon you" (Response)

✦ **Labas?** – "How are you?"

✦ **Bikhir, hamdulillah** – "I'm fine, thank God"

TIP:

Never rush a greeting—taking time to exchange pleasantries is a sign of respect.

2. DRESS CODE AND MODESTY

Morocco is a **Muslim-majority country**, and while major cities like **Marrakech and Casablanca** are more relaxed, modest dress is still appreciated, especially in **rural areas and religious sites**.

FOR WOMEN:

✦ Loose-fitting clothes that cover the **shoulders, chest, and knees** are best.

✦ A **scarf is not required**, except when visiting mosques.

FOR MEN:

✦ Shorts are generally fine, but **long pants are better** in conservative areas.

✦ Avoid **tank tops** outside beach towns.

BEACHWEAR:

✦ Bikinis are acceptable at **resorts and tourist beaches**, but it's polite to cover up when walking outside beach areas.

TIP:

A lightweight **scarf or shawl** is useful for covering up when needed.

A fragrant Moroccan dish

Moroccan meals are a **social and communal experience**, often shared from a **large central dish**.

EATING WITH HANDS:

✦ Moroccans traditionally eat with their **right hand** (the left is considered unclean).

✦ Use **bread instead of utensils** to scoop up food.

✦ If utensils are provided, use a **spoon for soups and a fork for couscous**.

GUEST ETIQUETTE:

✦ If invited to a **Moroccan home**, bring **small gifts** like sweets or nuts.

✦ Before eating, wait for the host to **say "Bismillah" (In the name of God)** before starting.

✦ It is polite to **accept a second serving**—this shows appreciation for the meal.

MUST-TRY MOROCCAN DISHES:

✦ **Tagine:** Slow-cooked stew with meat, vegetables, and spices.

✦ **Couscous:** A traditional Friday meal, served with vegetables and sauce.

✦ **Pastilla:** A flaky pastry filled with chicken or pigeon, almonds, and cinnamon.

✦ **Harira:** A hearty soup made with tomatoes, lentils, and chickpeas, often eaten during Ramadan.

TIP:

Always **compliment the cook—** saying **"Bsahtak"** (to your health) is appreciated.

4. TEA CULTURE IN MOROCCO

Tea is an important part of Moroccan hospitality

Tea, particularly **mint tea**, is an **important part of Moroccan hospitality**. It is offered to guests as a **symbol of welcome and friendship**.

How to Drink Moroccan Tea:

✦ It is usually **poured from a height** to create foam.

✦ The first glass is the **strongest**, and each refill gets **lighter**.

✦ It is **sweetened with sugar**—if you prefer less sugar, let your host know in advance.

TIP:

Never refuse tea when offered— it is considered **rude**. Even if you take just a sip, accepting it shows respect.

Colorful items sold at an open-air market

Moroccan souks (markets) are **a lively part of the culture**, offering everything from **handmade carpets to spices and leather goods**.

BARGAINING IS EXPECTED:

✦ Start by **offering half** the seller's first price and negotiate from there.

✦ Bargaining should be **friendly and respectful**—don't get frustrated.

✦ If you don't agree on a price, **politely walk away**—many sellers will call you back with a better offer.

COMMON SOUVENIR ITEMS:

✦ **Handmade rugs** – Berber carpets are famous for their unique designs.

✦ **Leather goods** – Essaouira and Fes have excellent tanneries.

✦ **Spices** – Saffron, cumin, and ras el hanout (a spice blend) are great choices.

✦ **Argan oil** – Available in cooperatives near Essaouira.

TIP:

Always **check the quality** of items before buying—some sellers try to pass off mass-produced goods as handmade.

6. RELIGION AND RESPECTING LOCAL CUSTOMS

Islam is deeply woven into Moroccan life. Even though Morocco is **relatively moderate**, it's important to **respect local religious customs**.

MOSQUES:

✦ **Non-Muslims cannot enter most mosques** except for the **Hassan II Mosque in Casablanca**.

✦ Always **dress modestly** if visiting religious sites.

RAMADAN:

✦ During Ramadan, many Moroccans **fast from sunrise to sunset**.

✦ While tourists are not required to fast, it's polite to **avoid eating, drinking, or smoking in public** during daylight hours.

✦ Restaurants in tourist areas remain open, but **smaller cafes may close until sunset**.

TIP:

If you hear the **call to prayer (ad-han)**, step aside briefly as a sign of respect.

7. GENDER AND SOCIAL INTERACTIONS

PUBLIC DISPLAYS OF AFFECTION:

✦ **Holding hands is fine**, but kissing and hugging in public is frowned upon.

✦ Couples should **avoid overly affectionate gestures** in conservative areas.

WOMEN TRAVELERS:

✦ Morocco is **safe for female travelers**, but **dressing modestly helps minimize unwanted attention**.

✦ In markets or busy streets, **firmly ignoring catcallers** is the best approach.

TIP:

If traveling solo, **sitting in cafés with other women** can help avoid unwanted attention.

8. TIPPING IN MOROCCO

Tipping is customary in Morocco and is **appreciated for most services**.

- **Cafés and Restaurants: 10% of the bill** if service is not included.
- **Taxi Drivers:** Round up the fare or tip **5-10 MAD** for short rides.
- **Tour Guides: 50-100 MAD per day**, depending on the service.
- **Hotel Staff: 10-20 MAD** for luggage handling or housekeeping.

TIP:

Keep **small change (dirhams)** handy for tipping, as many places **do not accept cards**.

FINAL THOUGHTS ON MOROCCAN CULTURE & ETIQUETTE

Morocco is a country of **rich traditions, deep hospitality, and strong cultural values**. By respecting local customs, dressing appropriately, and engaging with **warmth and curiosity**, you'll have a **more meaningful and rewarding travel experience**. In the next chapter, we'll explore **Morocco's 20 Must-See Locations**, from ancient medinas to hidden gems.

11

TOP 20 MUST-SEE LOCATIONS IN MOROCCO

Morocco is a country of diverse landscapes, ancient cities, and hidden gems. From the bustling souks of Marrakech to the vast dunes of the Sahara, there are countless places to explore. Whether you're drawn to history, nature, or adventure, this list highlights 20 must-see destinations that showcase Morocco's rich culture and beauty.

1. JEMAA EL-FNAA (MARRAKECH)

Marrakech's famous **main square** is a **UNESCO World Heritage Site** and the beating heart of the city. By day, it's filled with juice vendors, snake charmers, and street performers. By night, it transforms into a vibrant food market with music, storytellers, and lively crowds.

Best Time to Visit: Sunset, when the square comes alive.

Must-Do: Enjoy a traditional **harira soup and fresh orange juice** from a food stall.

Jemaa el-Fnaa

2. THE BLUE MEDINA OF CHEFCHAOUEN

Chefchaouen

Nestled in the **Rif Mountains**, Chefchaouen's **blue-painted streets** make it one of Morocco's most **picturesque and peaceful towns**. The medina is filled with **colorful doors, charming cafés, and craft shops**.

Best View: Hike to the **Spanish Mosque** for a panoramic view of the blue city.

Must-Do: Wander through the **blue alleyways** early in the morning for the best photos.

3. HASSAN II MOSQUE (CASABLANCA)

A beautiful fountain seen outside the mosque

One of the world's **largest mosques**, the **Hassan II Mosque** is an architectural masterpiece, set dramatically over the **Atlantic Ocean**.

Entrance Fee: 130 MAD (non-Muslim visitors allowed on guided tours).

Must-Do: Admire the **stunning mosaics, marble floors, and the second tallest minaret in the world (210m)**.

4. FES EL-BALI (FES)

A leather tannery seen at Chouara

The **oldest medina in Morocco**, Fes el-Bali is a **maze of 9,000 alleyways** filled with **souks, mosques, and madrasas**.

Must-Do: Visit **Al Quaraouiyine University**, the world's **oldest university**.

Best View: Climb to the rooftop terraces overlooking the **Chouara Tannery**.

5. THE SAHARA DESERT (MERZOUGA & ERG CHEBBI)

The **golden dunes of Erg Chebbi** offer an unforgettable desert experience.

Must-Do: Ride a **camel at sunset** and spend the night in a **Berber desert camp**.

Best Time to Visit: Spring and autumn for mild temperatures.

6. AÏT BEN HADDOU

A **UNESCO-listed ksar**, Aït Ben Haddou is one of Morocco's best-preserved **fortified villages**, used as a backdrop in movies and TV shows.

Must-Do: Walk through the ancient **mud-brick houses and climb to the granary** for incredible views.

Best Time to Visit: Early morning or late afternoon to avoid tour groups.

7. THE TODRA GORGE

Todra Gorge

A dramatic **limestone canyon** with **300-meter-high cliffs**, perfect for hiking and rock climbing.

Must-Do: Walk through the **narrowest part of the gorge** and visit a **traditional Berber village**.

Best Time to Visit: Morning for cooler temperatures and fewer crowds.

8. THE DADES VALLEY

A village situated in Dades Valley

Known as the **"Road of a Thousand Kasbahs,"** the Dades Valley features **winding mountain roads, dramatic rock formations, and ancient fortresses**.

Must-Do: Drive the **famous switchback road** and visit the **Monkey Fingers rock formations**.

Best Time to Visit: Spring, when the valley is lush and green.

9. THE KASBAH OF THE UDAYAS (RABAT)

Overlooking the Atlantic Ocean, this **white-and-blue kasbah** is one of Rabat's most beautiful spots.

Must-Do: Explore the **Andalusian Gardens** and enjoy **mint tea at Café Maure**.

Best Time to Visit: Late afternoon for stunning ocean views.

10. THE CORNICHE & BEACHFRONT (CASABLANCA)

Casablanca's **coastal promenade** offers stunning ocean views, cafés, and beach clubs.

Must-Do: Walk along the **Corniche** and visit **Ain Diab Beach**.

Best for: Sunset strolls and fresh seafood.

11. OUZOUD WATERFALLS

Ouzoud Waterfalls

The **tallest waterfalls in Morocco** (110m), surrounded by lush olive groves and wild monkeys.

Must-Do: Take a **boat ride to the base of the falls** and hike to the **top for panoramic views**.

Best Time to Visit: Spring and early summer for strong water flow.

12. THE ATLAS MOUNTAINS & IMLIL

The gateway to **Mount Toubkal**, North Africa's highest peak.

Must-Do: Hike through **Berber villages**, visit local markets, and stay in a **traditional guesthouse**.

Best Time to Visit: Spring and autumn for mild temperatures.

13. ESSAOUIRA – THE COASTAL GEM

A scene from the beach at Essaouira

A laid-back seaside town known for **its historic port, blue boats, and strong winds** (great for windsurfing).

Must-Do: Explore the **Skala de la Ville** ramparts and enjoy **grilled seafood at the port**.

Best Time to Visit: Summer for beach activities, spring and autumn for fewer crowds.

14. VOLUBILIS – ROMAN RUINS

Morocco's **best-preserved Roman site**, with stunning **mosaics, columns, and an ancient basilica**.

Must-Do: Walk through the ruins and see the **Triumphal Arch**.

Best Time to Visit: Morning for cooler weather.

15. THE RIF MOUNTAINS

The Rif Mountains

A less-explored region perfect for **hiking, nature lovers, and traditional Berber villages**.

Must-Do: Hike in **Talassemtane National Park** and visit **Akchour Waterfalls**.

16. SIDI IFNI

Sidi Ifni

A relaxed **coastal town with Spanish colonial architecture and stunning beaches**.

Must-Do: Visit **Legzira Beach**, famous for its **rock arch formations**.

17. AGADIR & TAGHAZOUT

Taghazout

A modern beach destination with a **laid-back surf town vibe**.

Must-Do: Take **surfing lessons** in Taghazout and enjoy the **sunset at Agadir's marina**.

18. EL JADIDA

A former **Portuguese settlement**, known for its **UNESCO-listed Cistern** and **fortified walls**.

Must-Do: Explore the **underground cistern**, one of Morocco's most unique sites.

19. THE MELLAH (JEWISH QUARTER) OF FES

Inside the Ibn Danan Synagogue

The **Mellah of Fes** is one of Morocco's most historic Jewish quarters, dating back to the 15th century. Once home to a thriving Jewish community, it features **narrow streets, unique architecture, and historic synagogues** that offer insight into Morocco's diverse cultural heritage.

Must-Do: Visit the **Ibn Danan Synagogue**, one of the oldest synagogues in North Africa, and explore the **Jewish cemetery**, known for its distinct white tombstones.

Best Time to Visit: Morning, when the streets are lively but not too crowded.

Pro Tip: Look for **traditional wooden balconies**, a unique feature of Mellah architecture.

20. SKOURA OASIS

Skoura

A **hidden gem** filled with **palm groves, ancient kasbahs, and lush gardens**.

Must-Do: Stay in a **traditional kasbah hotel** and explore the oasis on foot or bike.

FINAL THOUGHTS

From ancient cities to desert landscapes and coastal escapes, Morocco offers **a lifetime of experiences**. Whether you're exploring the **blue streets of Chefchaouen, hiking in the Atlas Mountains, or riding camels in the Sahara**, each destination tells a unique story.

In the next chapter, we'll discover **the top photography spots in Morocco**, capturing the country's beauty through the lens.

CHAPTER

12

BEST PLACES FOR PHOTOGRAPHY IN MOROCCO

Morocco is one of the most visually stunning destinations in the world, offering endless opportunities for photographers. From vibrant souks and ancient medinas to golden sand dunes and blue-washed alleyways, every corner of Morocco is a photographer's dream. Whether you're a professional photographer or a casual traveler, this guide will help you find the best locations to capture Morocco's beauty.

1. JEMAA EL-FNAA (MARRAKECH) – CAPTURING THE CHAOS

Marrakech's **iconic square** is one of the most vibrant places in Morocco. By day, it's filled with **snake charmers, juice vendors, and market stalls**. By night, it transforms into a sea of **food stalls, street musicians, and performers**.

Jemaa el-Fnaa

Best Time to Shoot: Sunset, when the sky turns golden, and the square is at its liveliest.

Best Viewpoint: Rooftop cafés like **Café de France or Le Grand Balcon du Café Glacier.**

Pro Tip: Use a **fast shutter speed** to capture the movement of performers and crowds.

2. THE BLUE STREETS OF CHEFCHAOUEN – A COLORFUL DREAM

Chefchaouen, known as **"The Blue Pearl,"** is one of the most **photogenic cities in the world**. Every street, staircase, and doorway is painted in **shades of blue**, creating an otherworldly atmosphere.

Best Time to Shoot: Early morning to avoid crowds.

BEST SPOTS:

✦ **The Blue Staircase** (near the Outa el Hammam Square).

✦ **The narrow alleyways leading to the medina gates**.

Pro Tip: Use a **wide-angle lens** to capture the narrow blue streets.

3. THE SAHARA DESERT (ERG CHEBBI & ERG CHIGAGA) – ENDLESS SAND DUNES

Erg Chebbi seen from Merzouga

The **Sahara Desert** is the ultimate location for capturing **golden sand dunes, camel caravans, and breathtaking sunsets**. The play of light and shadow on the dunes creates stunning compositions.

Best Time to Shoot: Sunset and sunrise, when the sand glows in shades of orange and gold.

BEST SPOTS:

+ **The high dunes of Erg Chebbi (Merzouga).**
+ **The remote dunes of Erg Chigaga.**

Pro Tip: Use a **telephoto lens** to capture the contrast between camels and dunes.

4. THE CHOUARA TANNERY (FES) – A BURST OF COLOR

Fes is home to **one of the oldest leather tanneries in the world**, where large stone vats are filled with **natural dyes in red, yellow, and blue**.

Best Time to Shoot: Late morning, when the sun is high and illuminates the dye vats.

Best Viewpoint: Rooftop terraces of the leather shops surrounding the tannery.

Pro Tip: Bring **mint leaves** to help with the strong smell of the tannery.

5. AÏT BEN HADDOU – A MOVIE-LIKE KASBAH

Aït Ben Haddou is a **UNESCO-listed fortress village** that looks like it belongs in a film—and in fact, it has been featured in movies such as **The Mummy**.

Best Time to Shoot: Sunrise or late afternoon, when the **red mud-brick walls glow in the sun**.

Best Viewpoint: The **hilltop granary** for a panoramic shot of the entire kasbah.

Pro Tip: Capture the **contrast between the kasbah's ancient architecture and the surrounding palm groves**.

6. THE TODRA AND DADES GORGES – DRAMATIC LANDSCAPES

Todra Gorge

These two **stunning rock canyons** in the Atlas Mountains provide some of Morocco's most breathtaking natural scenery.

Best Time to Shoot: Early morning, when light creates dramatic shadows on the canyon walls.

BEST SPOTS:

✦ **The narrowest part of Todra Gorge**, where the cliffs rise nearly 300 meters high.

✦ **The famous curvy road in Dades Gorge.**

Pro Tip: Use a **tripod for long-exposure shots** in the canyon's low light.

7. THE HASSAN II MOSQUE (CASABLANCA) – GRAND ARCHITECTURE

The **largest mosque in Morocco** is a masterpiece of Islamic architecture, featuring intricate tilework, an enormous prayer hall, and a minaret that towers **210 meters high**.

Best Time to Shoot: Sunset, when the **mosque is illuminated by golden light**.

Best Viewpoint: The mosque's **esplanade, where you can capture its full grandeur**.

Pro Tip: Use a **wide-angle lens** to emphasize the scale of the mosque.

8. ESSAOUIRA – THE BLUE BOATS AND COASTAL VIBES

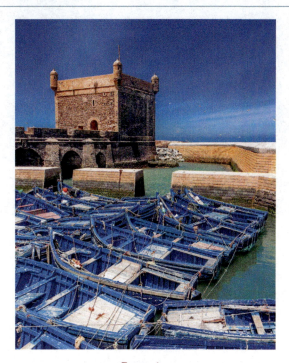

Essaouira

Essaouira's **fishing port, historic ramparts, and crashing waves** create a perfect setting for photography.

Best Time to Shoot: Early morning for golden light and fewer crowds.

✦   **The Skala de la Ville ramparts**, with its old cannons.

✦   **The blue fishing boats in the harbor.**

Pro Tip: Use **a polarizing filter** to enhance the blue tones of the boats and sky.

9. OUZOUD WATERFALLS – A NATURAL WONDER

A young visitors admires the waterfalls

The **tallest waterfalls in Morocco** (110m) are surrounded by lush greenery and are home to wild **Barbary macaques**.

Best Time to Shoot: Mid-morning, when the sun lights up the waterfalls.

Best Viewpoint: From the **bottom of the falls**, looking up.

Pro Tip: Use a **slow shutter speed to create a silky water effect**.

10. THE SOUKS OF MARRAKECH

Colorful spices and dyes seen at a souk in Marrakech

The **souk (market) of Marrakech** is a chaotic yet mesmerizing place to capture the essence of Moroccan life.

Best Time to Shoot: Late afternoon, when warm light filters through the market alleys.

BEST SUBJECTS:

✦ **Spice stalls with colorful powders in cone-shaped piles.**

✦ **Lantern shops glowing with golden light.**

Pro Tip: Politely ask vendors before taking their photo and offer a small tip if requested.

BONUS: BEST PHOTOGRAPHY TIPS FOR MOROCCO

+ **Use natural light:** Morocco's **golden hour** (just after sunrise and before sunset) creates warm, rich tones.

+ **Be respectful:** Always **ask permission before photographing people, especially in rural areas**.

+ **Pack multiple lenses:** A **wide-angle lens** for landscapes and architecture, and a **zoom lens** for portraits and street photography.

+ **Capture details:** Morocco's beauty is in its **intricate tiles, colorful textiles, and ornate doorways**—don't just focus on big landmarks.

+ **Be patient:** Markets and squares are busy—wait for the perfect moment when the scene aligns.

FINAL THOUGHTS ON PHOTOGRAPHY IN MOROCCO

Morocco offers **a world of color, texture, and light**, making it a dream destination for photographers. Whether you're capturing the **golden dunes of the Sahara, the chaos of Marrakech, or the quiet blue streets of Chefchaouen**, every shot tells a unique story.

In the next chapter, we'll dive into **essential Moroccan Arabic (Darija) survival phrases** to help you communicate and connect with locals during your journey.

BONUS CHAPTER: USEFUL MOROCCAN ARABIC (DARIJA) SURVIVAL PHRASES

> Moroccan Arabic, known as Darija, is the everyday spoken language in Morocco. While French is widely understood in cities, and English is common in tourist areas, learning a few key phrases in Darija will help you connect with locals and enhance your travel experience.

Moroccans appreciate any effort to speak their language, and even a simple **"Salam!" (Hello!)** can go a long way in showing respect and friendliness. This chapter covers **essential words and phrases** for greetings, shopping, transportation, dining, and more.

1. BASIC GREETINGS AND POLITENESS

Salam alaikum – "Peace be upon you" (*Common greeting*)

Wa alaikum salam – "And peace be upon you" (*Response to above*)

Labas? – "How are you?"

Bikhir, hamdulillah – "I'm fine, thanks be to God" (*Response to Labas?*)

Shukran – "Thank you"

Afak – "Please"

Smah liya – "Excuse me / Sorry"

Naam – "Yes"

La – "No"

Mafhemtsh – "I don't understand"

Kayn chi wahd kayhder Ingliziyya? – "Does anyone speak English?"

TIP:

Saying **"Shukran bzaf"** (Thank you very much) makes your gratitude sound extra polite.

2. NUMBERS (FOR SHOPPING AND MONEY)

1 – Wahed

2 – Jouj

3 – Tlata

4 – Rabaa

5 – Khamsa

6 – Seta

7 – Sebaa

8 – Tmnya

9 – Tesaa

10 – Aashra

Miya – "100"

Alf – "1,000"

Dirham – Moroccan currency

Example:

✦ **"Bsh-hal hadi?"** – "How much is this?"

✦ **"Hadi ghaliya bzaf!"** – "This is too expensive!"

✦ **"Nqes shwiya, afak?"** – "Can you lower the price, please?"

> **TIP:**
>
> Bargaining is normal in Moroccan markets, so don't be afraid to negotiate!

3. TRANSPORTATION AND DIRECTIONS

Fin kayn... ? – "Where is... ?"

Ana baghi nmshi l... – "I want to go to..."

Shhal taman? – "How much is the fare?"

Nqes shwiya, afak – "Lower the price a little, please" (*For taxis or market haggling*)

Wqaf hna, afak – "Stop here, please"

Sir nimna – "Go right"

Sir niss – "Go straight"

Sir nishta – "Go straight ahead"

Sir lisar – "Go left"

Trankil! – "Take it easy!" (*Used casually if someone is rushing*)

> **TIP:**
>
> **Petite taxis do not have set prices**—always agree on a fare before starting your ride or ask the driver to use the meter.

4. AT A RESTAURANT OR CAFÉ

Bghit menu, afak – "Can I have the menu, please?"

Ash kayn f'tayab? – "What do you have today?"

Bghit wahed tagine / couscous / harira – "I'd like a tagine / couscous / harira"

Ma bghitsh lhm – "I don't want meat" (*Useful for vegetarians*)

L'ma afak – "Water, please"

Shhal taman? – "How much is the bill?"

Sahha! – "Enjoy your meal!" (*Also means "cheers" or "to your health"*)

> **TIP:**
>
> Restaurants don't always bring the check automatically—say **"Afak, jibli l'adad"** ("Please bring me the bill").

5. EMERGENCY AND HEALTH PHRASES

Aji l'hna! – "Come here!" (*For calling for help*)

Kayn shi tabib? – "Is there a doctor?"

Ana mrid(a) – "I am sick"

Bghit shi dwa – "I need some medicine"

Tlef l'jawaz safar dyali! – "I lost my passport!"

Fin kayn l'bosta? – "Where is the police station?"

> **TIP:**
>
> If you need urgent help, dial **19 for police, 15 for an ambulance, and 150 for tourist police.**

6. PHRASES FOR MAKING FRIENDS

Smeh liya, nta/ntee mnin? – "Excuse me, where are you from?"

Ana mn... – "I am from..."

Bghit nt3lm Darija – "I want to learn Moroccan Arabic"*

Nti/Nta mzian(a) bzaf! – "You are very nice!"

Ana kanhbb l'Maghreb! – "I love Morocco!"

Choukran 3la l'hospitalité dyalkom – "Thank you for your hospitality"*

> **TIP:**
>
> Moroccans are very social and love to chat—don't be shy about starting a conversation!

* In Moroccan Arabic (Darija), the number **"3"** represents the Arabic letter ع ('ayn), a sound that doesn't exist in English, making it easier for non-Arabic speakers to pronounce words more accurately.

7. FUN SLANG WORDS & EXPRESSIONS

Mzyan! – "Great!" / "Good!"

Bzaf – "A lot / Very much"

Yallah! – "Let's go!"

Kif kif – "Same thing"

Wakha – "Okay / Alright"

Safi – "Enough / That's it"

Zwin(a)! – "Beautiful!"

> **TIP:**
>
> These phrases help you sound more like a local!

FINAL THOUGHTS ON MOROCCAN ARABIC (DARIJA)

You don't need to be fluent in Darija to **enjoy Morocco and connect with locals**, but knowing **a few key phrases** can **enhance your travel experience and show respect**. Moroccans appreciate when visitors try to speak their language, and even **simple greetings can open doors to great conversations and friendships**.

In the next section, we'll provide an **Appendix with references to key locations from previous chapters**, helping you plan your trip efficiently!

APPENDIX: QUICK REFERENCE GUIDE TO KEY LOCATIONS

This appendix provides an easy-to-navigate reference to the key locations mentioned throughout this guide. Whether you're planning your itinerary, looking for the best cities to visit, or revisiting a specific chapter, this section will help you quickly find the information you need.

1. MAJOR CITIES AND REGIONS

Destination	Chapter	Highlights
Marrakech	Chapter 3	Jemaa el-Fnaa, Bahia Palace, Majorelle Garden, Koutoubia Mosque
Fes	Chapter 4	Fes el-Bali, Al Quaraouiyine University, Chouara Tannery, Bou Inania Madrasa
Sahara Desert	Chapter 5	Erg Chebbi, Erg Chigaga, Camel trekking, Desert camping
Chefchaouen	Chapter 6	The blue medina, Spanish Mosque, Plaza Uta el-Hammam
Casablanca	Chapter 7	Hassan II Mosque, The Corniche, Art Deco district
Rabat	Chapter 7	Hassan Tower, Kasbah of the Udayas, Chellah ruins
Essaouira	Chapter 8	The Skala, Blue fishing boats, Surfing, Seafood markets
High Atlas Mountains	Chapter 9	Imlil, Mount Toubkal, Aït Bouguemez, Todra Gorge
Aït Ben Haddou	Chapter 9	UNESCO kasbah, Famous film location, Mud-brick architecture

2. NATURAL LANDMARKS AND OUTDOOR ADVENTURES

Landmark	Chapter	Highlights
Sahara Desert	Chapter 5	Camel trekking, Sand dunes, Stargazing, Berber camps
Todra Gorge	Chapter 9	Rock climbing, Scenic hikes, River canyon
Dades Valley	Chapter 9	Winding roads, "Monkey Fingers" rock formations
Ouzoud Waterfalls	Chapter 9	Morocco's tallest waterfalls, Wild monkeys, Boat rides
Mount Toubkal	Chapter 9	Highest peak in North Africa, 2-day trek
Akchour Waterfalls	Chapter 6	Scenic hike near Chefchaouen, God's Bridge rock formation

3. HISTORICAL & CULTURAL LANDMARKS

Landmark	Chapter	Highlights
Jemaa el-Fnaa	Chapter 3	Lively night market, Food stalls, Street performers
Hassan II Mosque	Chapter 7	Largest mosque in Morocco, Overlooking the Atlantic
Aït Ben Haddou	Chapter 9	UNESCO-listed kasbah, Ancient Berber village
Al Quaraouiyine University	Chapter 4	World's oldest university, Fes medina
Kasbah of the Udayas	Chapter 7	Blue-and-white fortress, Ocean views
Volubilis	Chapter 11	Ancient Roman ruins, Well-preserved mosaics

4. BEST PLACES FOR PHOTOGRAPHY

Photo Location	Chapter	Best Feature
Chefchaouen Medina	Chapter 6	Blue-washed walls, Colorful doorways
Sahara Desert	Chapter 5	Golden dunes, Camel caravans at sunrise
Chouara Tannery (Fes)	Chapter 4	Vibrant dye vats, Leather artisans
Majorelle Garden (Marrakech)	Chapter 3	Exotic plants, Bold blue architecture
Aït Ben Haddou	Chapter 9	Ancient kasbah with desert backdrop
Essaouira Port	Chapter 8	Blue fishing boats, Historic fortress

5. BEST PLACES FOR FOOD LOVERS

City	Chapter	Must-Try Dishes
Marrakech	Chapter 3	Tanjia, Lamb tagine, Fresh orange juice
Fes	Chapter 4	Pastilla, Bissara, Traditional couscous
Essaouira	Chapter 8	Grilled seafood, Sardines, Fish tagine
Casablanca	Chapter 7	Fresh seafood, French-influenced Moroccan dishes
Rabat	Chapter 7	Harira soup, Street food stalls

6. KEY TRAVEL TIPS AND SURVIVAL PHRASES

Topic	Chapter	Key Information
Entry Requirements & Visas	Chapter 2	Visa-free for many countries, Passport must be valid for 6 months
Transportation	Chapter 2	Trains, Buses, Taxis, Airport transfers
Shopping & Bargaining	Chapter 10	Haggling is expected, Start at half the asking price
Moroccan Arabic (Darija) Phrases	Chapter 12	Common greetings, Numbers, Directions
Best Time to Visit Morocco	Introduction	Spring & Fall are ideal, Summers are hot inland

FINAL THOUGHTS

This appendix serves as a **quick reference** to help you navigate through Morocco's top locations, cultural experiences, and travel essentials. Whether you're **planning your itinerary, looking for the best places to take photos, or brushing up on local phrases**, this section ensures you have **all the key information at your fingertips**.

With this guide in hand, you're ready to **explore Morocco with confidence—** from the **ancient medinas of Fes and Marrakech** to the **golden dunes of the Sahara**. Enjoy your journey through one of the **most captivating countries in the world!**

Here's another book by Captivating Travels that you might like

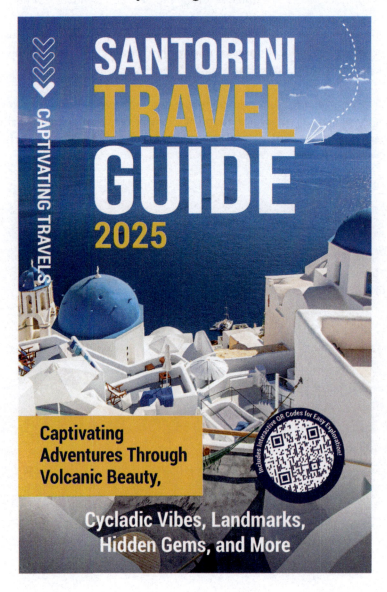

Welcome Aboard, Discover
Your Limited-Time Free Bonus!

Hello, traveler! Welcome to the Captivating Travels family, and thanks for grabbing a copy of this book! Since you've chosen to join us on this journey, we'd like to offer you something special.

Check out the link below for a FREE Ultimate Travel Checklist eBook & Printable PDF to make your travel planning stress-free and enjoyable.

But that's not all - you'll also gain access to our exclusive email list with even more free e-books and insider travel tips. Well, what are you waiting for? Click the link below to join and embark on your next adventure with ease.

Access your bonus here: https://livetolearn.lpages.co/checklist/
Or, Scan the QR code!

IMAGE SOURCES

1. www.openstreetmap.org

2. Photo by Harriet B.: https://www.pexels.com/photo/a-market-with-many-lamps-hanging-from-the-ceiling-18687094/

3. Sharon Hahn Darlin, CC BY 2.0 <https://creativecommons.org/licenses/by/2.0>, via Wikimedia Commons https://commons.wikimedia.org/wiki/File:Casablanca_Mohammed_V_International_Airport,_Morocco_January_2024_-_Exterior.jpg

4. RACHID BAYA, CC0, via Wikimedia Commons https://commons.wikimedia.org/wiki/File:AEROPORT_FES_SAISS_FES_Commune_Oulad_Tay.jpg

5. www.openstreetmap.org

6. Sidimomo, CC BY-SA 3.0 <https://creativecommons.org/licenses/by-sa/3.0>, via Wikimedia Commons https://commons.wikimedia.org/wiki/File:Rabat-Sal%C3%A9_airport.jpg

7. www.openstreetmap.org

8. Photo by Ayoub Moukhliss: https://www.pexels.com/photo/friends-enjoying-sunset-at-essaouira-seaside-29354398/

9. www.openstreetmap.org

10 Photo by Gül Işık: https://www.pexels.com/photo/cacti-outside-a-building-13794444/

11. www.openstreetmap.org

12 Bjørn Christian Tørrissen, CC BY-SA 3.0 <https://creativecommons.org/licenses/by-sa/3.0>, via Wikimedia Commons https://commons.wikimedia.org/wiki/File:Fes_Bab_Bou_Jeloud_2011.jpg

13 Bjørn Christian Tørrissen, CC BY-SA 3.0 <https://creativecommons.org/licenses/by-sa/3.0>, via Wikimedia Commons https://commons.wikimedia.org/wiki/File:Bou_Inania_Madrasa_2011.jpg

14. Robert Prazeres, CC BY-SA 4.0 <https://creativecommons.org/licenses/by-sa/4.0>, via Wikimedia Commons https://commons.wikimedia.org/wiki/File:Hamra_mosque_in_Fes_Jdid.jpg

15. *www.openstreetmap.org*

16. *www.openstreetmap.org*

17. *https://commons.wikimedia.org/w/index.php?curid=141139416*

18. *Yannaikashtan, CC BY-SA 4.0 <https://creativecommons.org/licenses/by-sa/4.0>, via Wikimedia Commons https://commons.wikimedia.org/wiki/File:Bridge_of_God.jpg*

19. *www.openstreetmap.org*

20. *www.openstreetmap.org*

21. *Rigelus, CC BY-SA 4.0 <https://creativecommons.org/licenses/by-sa/4.0>, via Wikimedia Commons https://commons.wikimedia.org/wiki/File:%D0%9F%D0%BB%D0%BE%D1%89%D0%B0%D0%B4%D1%8C_%D0%9C%D1%83%D1%85%D0%B0%D0%BC%D0%BC%D0%B5%D0%B4%D0%B0_V.jpg*

22. *Anass Sedrati, CC BY-SA 4.0 <https://creativecommons.org/licenses/by-sa/4.0>, via Wikimedia Commons https://commons.wikimedia.org/wiki/File:Inside_the_great_mosque_of_Sal%C3%A9.jpg*

23. *www.openstreetmap.org*

24. *Visions of Domino, CC BY 2.0 <https://creativecommons.org/licenses/by/2.0>, via Wikimedia Commons https://commons.wikimedia.org/wiki/File:Morocco_-_Essaouira_Part_2_(31679848385).jpg*

Printed in Great Britain
by Amazon

63122245R00087